METHODS OF MISSION
IN SOUTHERN AFRICA

METHODS OF MISSION
IN SOUTHERN AFRICA

BY

John Carter

WITH A
FOREWORD BY
The Most Reverend Joost de Blank
Archbishop of Cape Town

LONDON
S · P · C · K
1963

First published in 1963
by S.P.C.K.
Holy Trinity Church, Marylebone Road,
London N.W.1

Printed in Great Britain by
The Talbot Press (S.P.C.K.)
Saffron Walden, Essex

Contents

TO

F. G. S. C.
(Targe)

Introduction

The background of this book is South Africa. The point of view is Anglican. The book came into being because I was asked by the Provincial Board of Missionary Strategy to write something on methods of mission, "describing the work of the laity in evangelization, and showing the Church active in the world". For this reason it deals with the life and needs of the Church of the Province of South Africa, but I hope it may be of interest to Christians who do not share its particular background or its particular point of view, for the Christian mission concerns us all.

I would like to make it clear that what is written here is in no sense an official statement. It makes no claim to be exhaustive or definitive. It is merely a humble contribution to a conversation that ought to be going on all the time, and if it provokes others to read, think, and talk about the mission of the Church it will have done some good. One virtue I would claim for it, despite all its inadequacies : it is not a monologue. There are many voices here, for I have tried to quote those who can speak with the authority of experience. I want to thank all who have allowed me to use their words, though I must accept responsibility for the selection and presentation of the material.

In particular, I am indebted to the Reverend Cyprian Thorpe and the Reverend Alex King for much of the material in Chapter 5, and with them to the other members of the Board's Executive, not least to its Chairman, the Bishop of Grahamstown, and its Secretary, Canon F. A. Amoore, for helpful criticisms, suggestions, and encouragement. All who study the outreach of the Church in our time have reason to be grateful for the writings of the Archbishop of Cape Town, and in addition I am honoured by his Grace's contribution of a Foreword to this little book. Acknowledgements of literary sources are made wherever these sources have been traced. Where references have eluded me or ideas have become so assimilated that I have not been able to recognize a particular debt, I must ask to be forgiven.

Mission is a difficult subject because it is so wide. It involves everything from the Church's understanding of itself to the way the Gospel is expressed in words and actions. It is also difficult because it is so demanding. We have to face these difficulties because mission is our job—the job of the laity no less than of the clergy. It is only as we face them that the excitement of the Christian calling begins to grip us. If we find the way hard it is, perhaps, a sign that we are on the right track.

JOHN CARTER

Acknowledgements

Thanks are due to the following for permission to quote from copyright sources:

Church Army: *Schools of Evangelism.*

Church Information Office: *The Moving Spirit,* and *Towards the Conversion of England.*

James Clarke & Co., Ltd: *The Christian Message in a Non-Christian World,* by Hendrik Kraemer.

J. M. Dent & Sons, Ltd: "Bishops", by Raymond Mortimer, *Turnstile I.*

Edinburgh House Press: *The Christian Approach to the Animist,* by Geoffrey Parrinder, and *Creative Tension,* by Stephen Neill.

Faber & Faber, Ltd: *Liturgy and Society,* by A. G. Hebert, and *Theology and Society,* by V. A. Demant.

Canon F. Findley: "On Parish Magazines", *Good Hope,* July, 1962.

Guild of St Barnabas (South Africa): article by Anthony Barker, *Compassion,* No. 2, 1962.

Hodder & Stoughton, Ltd: *The Practice of Evangelism,* by Bryan Green.

Hutchinson & Co., Ltd: *Part-time Priests,* edited by Robin Denniston.

Industrial Christian Fellowship: *The Church and the Life of Fellowship,* by A. G. Hebert.

International Missionary Council, London: *One Body, one Gospel, one World,* by Lesslie Newbigin.

International Missionary Council, New York: *All-Africa Church Conference 1958: The Church in a Changing World.*

ACKNOWLEDGEMENTS

International Review of Missions: article by J. C. Hoekendijk, *I.R.M.*, 1952.

Longmans, Green & Co., Ltd: *Parochial Missions To-day*, by Peter Green.

Lutterworth Press, Ltd: *Bantu Prophets in South Africa*, by Bengt Sundkler. *Conflict and Agreement in the Church*, by T. F. Torrance, and *A Theology of the Laity*, by Hendrik Kraemer.

The Reverend Dr. George MacLeod: *Only One Way Left*.

Oxford University Press, Cape Town: *Townsmen or Tribesmen*, by Philip Mayer.

Oxford University Press, London: *The City of God*, by Edgar Brookes, and *William Temple*, by F. A. Iremonger.

Penguin Books, Ltd: *Christianity and Politics in Africa*, by J. V. Taylor, and *Christianity and Social Order*, by William Temple.

Routledge & Kegan Paul, Ltd: *The Historic Reality of Christian Culture*, by Christopher Dawson.

The Seabury Press: "The Church's Mission", by Bishop Lyman C. Ogilby, *Viewpoints*, edited by John W. Coburn & Norman Pittenger.

Seven Seas Book Publishers: *Down Second Avenue*, by Ezekiel Mphahlele.

Student Christian Movement Press, Ltd: *The Bible in Our Time*, by E. H. Robertson, *Christians of the Copperbelt*, by J. V. Taylor & Dorothea Lehmann, *Florence Allshorn*, by J. H. Oldham, *The Jesus of History*, by T. R. Glover, *Life is Commitment*, by J. H. Oldham, *The Liturgical Movement and the Local Church*, by A. Shands, *Local Church and World Mission*, by Douglas Webster, *Processes of Growth in an African Church*, by J. V. Taylor, *Revival*, by M. A. C. Warren, and *The Reunion of the Church*, by Lesslie Newbigin.

Survey Application Trust: *Missionary Methods—St Paul's or Ours?* by Roland Allen.

World Council of Churches: *Signs of Renewal*.

World Student Christian Federation: "Christ's Ministry to the World", by P. Maury, and "The Triune God, Mission and Unity", by D. T. Niles, in *The Student World*, nos. 1-2, 1961.

Foreword

This book was conceived within a South African environment and written out of the experience and knowledge accumulated in the southern tip of Africa. It is important in its dealing with many of our contemporary problems and by addressing itself to our present situation. Nothing could be more necessary for our people than to make certain that we have really reached the end of paternalism, and that we meet as equals and not as master and servant or as missionary and primitive tribesman.

Similarly, there can be no doubt that the missionary work of the Church in South Africa to-day is bedevilled (this is the only proper word to use in the circumstances) by the official racial policies so zealously initiated and pursued by the authorities. There can be little surprise that much of the population is being lost to Islam or agnosticism when it is patent for all to see that the Christian Faith is interpreted largely in western terms, and that its benefits are primarily for the white *"herrenvolk"*. Not until all vestige of discrimination on the grounds of colour alone has been expunged from the statute books and the practice of the people of our land can the Word of God have free course and be glorified. Moreover, white domination or white superiority breeds black nationalism and black superiority. And having sown the wind in many parts of Africa, the white man is finding to his cost that he is reaping the whirl-wind. Such a diabolical policy as white authoritarianism has its own doom written within itself. Its *hybris* brings its own inevitable *nemesis*.

John Carter's book is therefore a revealing study of conditions in South Africa to-day and a call to all Christians everywhere to work for the end of segregation among the races on a "holier" or "better" or a "more educated than thou" basis. All men are made in God's image. All Christians set their eternal hope not on the accident of racial blood but in the Redeeming Blood of Christ, not on the fact of birth in this nation or that, but on the miracle of Rebirth—a Rebirth of water and the Holy Ghost.

But although I have frankly stated the South African context of *Methods of Mission* it would be quite wrong to think that the book's value is limited to the South African scene. Speaking from the African scene, but equally relevant everywhere, the author has set down the principles of missionary work in the world to-day. The need for lay activity (and often for lay leadership), the problem of communication, the need for effective literature—these and many similar points he brings to our notice and applies to all Christians wheresoever they may be.

The difficulties of effective communication are every whit as perplexing in the Britain of to-day as in the hinterland of Africa. Furthermore, the mobilization of the Parish in missionary prayer and endeavour is universal in its demand.

I am therefore convinced that there is no Christian man or woman who takes his faith seriously, who will not be stimulated and helped by this book. It is short enough to read quickly. And having read it, the reader of goodwill will wish to return to this or that section again and again

as it sums up for him the most pressing Christian require-
ments of the day and his own direct responsibility.

I believe this book is worthy of a large circulation both
inside South Africa and outside it. I believe if its contents
are taken seriously it will enlarge the Christian's vision and
drive him anew to deepen his own particular calling and
contribution. This is true of all Christians everywhere. I
pray its words may be widely disseminated and that they
may fall on to no ears grown deaf with complacency or
lack of exercise. This book within the evangelistic context
may well be God's Word to us at this time. As we hear,
may we be eager to obey.

✠ JOOST CAPETOWN

1

The Mission of the Church

THE word "mission" is often in the newspaper headlines. Prime Ministers and Foreign Secretaries, as they cross the world to meet in Geneva or Moscow or New York, are men with a mission. "Business missions" arrive by jet-liner and are welcomed with V.I.P. treatment. Anybody sent out with a job to do—particularly if it is an important job— may be spoken of as having a mission. For "mission" simply means "sending".

In the armed forces of the United States the word is used a great deal, both to describe the "terms of reference" of a particular unit or base, and also to denote a single sortie or military operation. The pilot coming home radios "mission completed", as he inserts another wedge of chewing-gum behind the toothpaste smile. Cinema addicts know the scene by heart.

"Mission" is a handy word, but because it is used in so many ways we have to be sure what we mean by it. Christians use it too—they have been using it for hundreds of years. And there is often some confusion or uncertainty about its meaning.

It is a long time since Church-members in the West became accustomed to speaking of "foreign missions" as distinct from "home missions"—so long that a person in Europe or America who says he is "interested in missions" would now generally be assumed to be thinking of the work

1

of the Church overseas. Police courts may still have their "missionary" to help with the rehabilitation of offenders, but this word, too, came to be applied chiefly to people doing work in foreign lands.

All this is rather confusing when you are on the receiving end—and particularly when you realize that the receiving end has itself become a sending end. Missionaries may be of any nationality or race or colour, and may work within their homeland or outside it. But the principle remains the same : they are those who are sent. And the title of "missionary" is surely too good to lose : certainly it is to be preferred to the mealy-mouthed "fraternal worker".

Again, people talk of a parish "having a Mission", and it may be a parish of any kind in any country. Here the context usually supplies the clue : the reference is to a short, intensive period of evangelistic activity.

The key-thought behind all these expressions is the thought of "sending". Christians to-day are learning to see all the varieties and examples of mission as parts of *one* mission. They speak more often of mission in the singular, and they mean the permanent purpose of the Church in the world. For the Church is on duty. It has a job to do. So, when we talk of Parish Missions or University Missions or Industrial Missions we try to see them as temporary or special embodiments of the one constant purpose.

We shall probably go on using the old words. But as we do so we may find it necessary to think out their meaning afresh. For when Christians talk of "mission" they are talking of *their own involvement in the most important job in the world*. And in a changing world we have to be sure that there is no time-lag in our thinking.

Can our job really be more important than the "missions" of the statesmen, the captains of industry, and the captains of aircraft, even in a day when these are the men who can order, produce, and deliver the hydrogen bomb? Yes; for this job of ours is something that involves all mankind and all creation, and it is concerned not with temporal survival only but with the very purpose for which men and things were made.

The Christian mission has been defined as "the redemptive activity of God in the world through the Church".[1] This mission springs from the nature of God himself. He is the living God, active and outgoing in love. Man is made for God, and man is meant to be "the priest of creation", through whom the whole order of things is to find a voice and a self-consciousness.

But it is the fact of sin that conditions our mission now, and unless we take very seriously the separation that sin has caused between man and God and between man and man, we cannot begin to understand what it is that we are called to do. Sin infects the whole created order. It has to be dealt with in man, and the whole creation waits for this to happen, groaning in a universal travail (Rom. 8. 22).

Man has to be rescued from himself by God's great act in history, which begins with the call of Abraham, continues in the giving of the Law and the message of the Prophets, and reaches its decisive climax in the birth, life, death, and resurrection of Christ.

The needs of men are a motive for mission, but only because in Christ we are given the answer to those needs: only because in him is the way of at-one-ment. Christians have a Gospel—good news, not just good advice. It is good news for all mankind, and the obligation is laid upon us to pass it on. "The good news is that God, the source, the end,

3

and the Lord of the created world, is by his own divine initiative active to restore things to their true nature, and invites men to enter into this stream of divine liberation." [2] The obligation is expressed simply and clearly in the statement : "Christ died for everybody, and everybody has a right to know." A thousand million people alive to-day do not know. Every generation has to be evangelized afresh, and every generation is bigger than the last.

All these motives for mission come to a point in the marching-orders of the risen Christ himself : "As the Father hath sent me, even so send I you" (John 20. 21). Pentecost marks the beginning of a new phase of mission, which continues to-day.

The principle of selection that runs through biblical history is a problem to many people. How odd of God to choose, not only the Jews, but the Christians too. But selection is always related to mission, and without mission it would indeed be odd, if not immoral. God works by calling some, that they may be the means of bringing his message to the rest; and Christians should know that they are called not for privilege but for service, not to be ingrowing but to be outgoing. In the words of William Temple : "If the Gospel is true for anyone, anywhere, it is true for all men everywhere : and the Church is *his* Church exactly in so far as it is carrying out its missionary task."

In this task every Christian is involved. But it is important to recognize that no part of God's action is individualistic. This is true of the redemptive process. Its purpose is the redemption of the world, not redemption *from* the world. The end is that all things may be gathered up in Christ. It is equally true of the Church as the redeeming community. Man is created to be the co-operator with God in a garden where everything is lovely,[3] and fallen man, redeemed in Christ, is to die to self that he may live to God and to his fellows.

The mission, in the Bible, is a corporate action : we are caught up in it with God and with others. So redeemed men, united with the Second Adam, become again fellow-workers with God—a New Israel, God's people and God's agents in the world. The missionary obligation is not an optional extra or a departmental affair. It is laid upon every Christian because it is laid upon the whole Church.

It is important, however, that we should not assume from this inescapable corollary a simple, easy identification of Church and mission. There used to be a convenient delusion that Church and mission were separable, the Church being our local comfort-station, and the mission being the concern of a number of full-time specialists "over there", supported by some of us who liked that sort of thing. It is rare to find anyone defending this position to-day, though it survives in the back of many people's minds. Now, we are told, the mission of the Church refers to its total task : "The Church *is* mission." We are all in it together. *The whole life of the Church in every parish and district is the agency of God's redemptive purpose to the world around.* For the Church is here to change the world, no less.

This is wonderful. It is a truly revolutionary insight—once it passes beyond the realm of words and begins to change us. The danger is that it will stay in the realm of words, and that our most complacent members will learn to say, "the Church is mission", while doing nothing whatever about it.

If this happens, the great phrase will be a great delusion. There is no easy transition from the old separation to the

5

new unity. Unless we are prepared to say "the Church is mission" with real penitence, and with a desire and readiness for renewal, service, and sacrifice, the revolutionary phrase will become a dangerous cliché. For to say that the Church is mission may bring out the fact that there is a missionary dimension to everything the Church does, but it may also conceal the fact that specific missionary actions are called for.[4] The loaf does not rise without the leaven.

This means that our thinking cannot now be woolly and general, on the excuse that all mission is one. We may accept unreservedly the unity and totality of mission, but we still have to express our missionary obedience in particular ways. There are great practical differences between the Church's outreach to the unevangelized masses of Africa, her fulfilment of her mission in established parishes, and her concern to penetrate and transform the working world of everyday life. These are three aspects of one mission, and they are very closely related. The differences between them are not differences of colour. An African parish has a missionary obligation to its unevangelized people, and so has a parish in a white suburb of Johannesburg. But each different area poses its own special problems, and it is only as we take these problems seriously that we shall begin to understand the revolutionary nature of the concept of the Church as mission.

In the same way, this new unity of thinking does not imply that no specific actions are called for. We shall not get anywhere unless we take particular steps. Bishop Stephen Neill said once, "If everything is mission, nothing is mission".[5] And Bishop Lesslie Newbigin, himself a great teacher of what it means that the Church is mission, sounded the same warning when he wrote : "Unless there is in the life of the Church *a point of concentration* for the missionary intention, the missionary dimension which is proper to the whole life of the Church will be lost. (One may compare, for instance, the familiar fact that one learns to regard all days as holy not by treating all days as equal, but by treating one day as holy, the 'Lord's Day'.)" [6]

A complacent Church is *not* mission. A Church which *is* mission will be restless and active. The Church must always be pressing out beyond its immediate horizon to pursue its great unfinished task. History shows the necessity for a prophetic initiative, renewed again and again, to rouse the Church and keep it on the move.

NOTES

1. Minute of the Provincial Board of Missionary Strategy, 22 February 1962.
2. Hendrik Kraemer, *A Theology of the Laity*, p. 93.
3. George Macleod, *Only One Way Left*, p. 29.
4. See: Lesslie Newbigin, *One Body, One Gospel, One World*, and Douglas Webster, *Missionary Societies—One or Many?*
5. Stephen Neill, *Creative Tension*, p. 81.
6. Lesslie Newbigin, *One Body, One Gospel, One World*, p. 43 (italics added).

2

The Missionary Movement

ONE of the clearest examples of this prophetic initiative is the modern missionary movement of the eighteenth and nineteenth centuries. It is a matter of history that at a time when the Church was asleep, prophetic individuals and groups took up the burden of world-evangelization. Hendrik Kraemer writes: "The 'Great Awakening' in America, the momentous Wesleyan revival in England, Pietism as a movement of religious regeneration on the Continent of Europe, constitute the spiritual soil from which this amazing outburst of world-embracing apostolic zeal sprang." [1]

The movement was largely, under God, the work of lay-men and of voluntary societies. Kraemer, pointing out that it happened mainly as a result of lay initiative, and was only, in its deployment, gradually recognized as the natural task of the Church, goes on to suggest that it was then too much clericalized.[2] But lay initiative continued to find an outlet in international, inter-confessional, and essentially missionary-hearted movements such as the Y.M.C.A., the Y.W.C.A., and the World Student Christian Federation. Kraemer says: "It cannot be too strongly stressed that these great expressions of Christian lay-vision and sense of responsibility have performed *vicariously* a task which in principle lies within the calling of the Church, but for which the Church as a whole was in the nineteenth century too clumsy, too defensive and empty of real vision." [3]

From the point of view of Anglican missionary work the eighteenth century is specially significant : our two greatest missionary societies were founded, one at its beginning, the other at its close. It is a measure of the faith of the founders that they had wide horizons. The declared aim of the Society for the Propagation of the Gospel in 1701 was not merely "to help our own people in the North American Colonies", but also "to convert the Nations". And the sixteen clergymen and nine laymen who founded the Church Missionary Society in 1799 took as their territory "Africa and the East".

If the element of voluntary initiative in Anglican missionary expansion was partly responsible for the old division between Church and mission it also had positive advantages. It ensured that the established Church in England did not conduct its expansion abroad as a department of state; it ensured that the faith spread outside areas of Britain's political control; and it ensured the development of autonomous Churches whose future was not bound up with that of the British Empire.[4]

To-day, in close operation with many other Anglican missionary agencies, and many Provinces and dioceses, the S.P.G. and C.M.S., having helped to plant the Church of Christ across the world, are engaged in fostering the fullness of its growth. Anglican missionaries are using the Bible in more than two hundred languages—a measure of the extent and variety of the Anglican Communion. Each new Province, owing its origin to missionary enterprise, becomes itself an agent in the missionary movement.

In this great development the Church of the Province of South Africa has shared, first as a beneficiary, more recently as a partner. We are now a Church with well over a million members, whose missionary responsibilities have been described in the following terms : "The Church of the Province of South Africa, which includes the Protectorates of Basutoland, Bechuanaland, and Swaziland, has no organized missionary work *outside* the borders of the Province. There is, however, a considerable volume of missionary work under the auspices of the Church of the Province among the Bantu peoples of the country. In this work considerable assistance is given by the S.P.G. and the Community of the Resurrection, the Society of the Sacred Mission, and the Society of St John the Evangelist, all from England." [5] The Church also has a missionary outreach among Muslims and Hindus, with a few specialized agencies such as the Diocesan Mission to Muslims in the Cape. She seeks to present the claims of Christ to all the people of South Africa.

The development of the Church of the Province, like that of the Anglican Communion in other parts of the world, has not followed the lines of a consciously unfolding strategy. The Church grew by tackling the obvious jobs, and these led on to others. When Robert Gray was consecrated first Bishop of Cape Town in 1847 there were only eleven clergymen and a dozen church buildings in an area of 110,000 square miles with an Anglican population of about 10,000. The Church followed her people, drawing them together and encouraging them to make the exertions and sacrifices necessary for the building up of parish life. Andrew Murray wrote of Bishop Gray, that great traveller : "He is exceedingly active and will not rest till he has churches everywhere." [6]

Problems of distance, as well as the need to reach out to the heathen, led to the formation of new dioceses. In one striking example, the diocese of Lebombo, we see the

Church deliberately following Africans who had been converted in the Transvaal back into their own territory, even though, in doing so, it "entered a foreign country, which had been occupied by people of another European race, and professing another form of the Christian faith, for hundreds of years".[7]

At the local level the growth of the Church appears to have been equally spontaneous. African catechists, many of them unpaid volunteers, began to plant the Church in scattered villages and kraals, which only later came to be reckoned part of a Mission District. This voluntary initiative is by no means a thing of the past. In 1958 the Bishop of Pretoria reported: "The spearhead of our evangelistic work is a company of about 400 voluntary catechists and sub-catechists, who in the absence of the clergy conduct services and take classes. The work of the Church in this large and scattered diocese has, in almost every instance, been started by these voluntary workers, who, having caught this love of our Lord Jesus Christ, go forth to preach it with enthusiasm and in many cases with real personal self-sacrifice. The hope for the future lies in the enthusiasm and devotion of these men and women." [8] Commenting on this, the Bishop of Grahamstown writes: "The diocese of Pretoria is a most glorious example of the way the Holy Spirit has worked; it can be compared to a veld fire which carries burning firebrands hither and thither."

Nothing can ever replace this personal participation in the Church's mission. Since Andrew first found his own brother, Peter, and brought him to Jesus, it has been the essential method behind all the methods. The picture we get of the early Church in the Acts of the Apostles is not that of a Church following a formal pattern of advance through a few appointed agents only. We can be sure that the sailor who became a Christian told his mates in the fo'c'sle and the people he met in foreign ports. The merchant travelling overland sold his goods, and gave away the Gospel as well. Aquila and Priscilla may have been among the first to take the good news to Rome, the capital of the civilized world. *Every* Christian was caught up in the mission of the Church. For when Christ changes people the process cannot stop there : redeemed men and women become ambassadors for Christ.

A million members of our Church, and more, are spread out through the whole life of South Africa. Each one is called to be a witness for our Lord, and, in the words of a classic definition, "so to present Christ Jesus in the power of the Holy Spirit, that men shall come to put their trust in God through him, to accept him as their Saviour, and serve him as their King in the fellowship of his Church".[9]

As time passes, Christian obedience tends to express itself through settled institutions. But we can never do without the personal commitment that makes every day of Christian living an adventure of faith. For the rank and file of Christ's army, there is no discharge in this war.

Recognition, toleration, and the establishment of institutions bring their own problems to the Christian Church. It is tempting to think that it must have been more exciting to be a Christian before the conversion of Constantine than after it. But to run back to the catacombs would be sheer evasion and escape; and in the same way the Church in South Africa must accept the responsibilities that its own growth and development have brought.

We can be proud of the great mission stations of the Transkei and Zululand, Ovamboland and the Transvaal, but we must never sit back and think the job is done. The acceptance by each Christian of his missionary responsibility remains vitally important. We can never forget that the Church exists not for its own sake, but for the world which God loved and which Christ died to save. And neither do we ever get beyond the reach of the question : *How* are we to fulfil the obligation that is laid upon us? In every generation men and women are to be drawn into the stream of divine liberation—but by what methods? The searching test of the "even so" in Christ's great commission must always be faced : our Lord's own incarnate life and ministry are the pattern.

Looking back down the long vista of Christian history, it is easy to pick out wrong methods in the past—methods which do not measure up to the "even so". The Crusades look pretty tarnished now, though the assumption behind them would not have been easily challenged at the time : Francis of Assisi and Raimon Lull were lonely figures in their day. We remember, too, how devout Christians of a later age defended the institution of slavery, and how some still defend race-discrimination.

The Church is bound to reject methods which are not true to the New Testament revelation. But also, the Church is bound to seek and to use methods that measure up to the needs of the contemporary situation.

Missionaries who have worked in China say that their own standard of life turned out to be a disadvantage, because it put a gulf between them and the great mass of the Chinese people. Churches, schools, and hospitals were not enough. Looking back, they wish they could somehow have identified themselves more fully with those whom they sought to serve. With penetrating hindsight, tragically too late to be of use to them (though not, perhaps, to others), they enumerate the lessons learned in China : Christians must be deeply grounded in theology; Christianity must be shown to be realistic, not merely idealistic; there must be a fellowship among Christians transcending race and class; the Church must become self-governing, self-supporting, and self-propagating; greater efforts must be made to increase the number of well-educated, experienced, and completely dedicated Christian leaders, not only in the cities but also in the villages; the Church should not be deluded by any sense of false security; Christians must avoid being forced into the position of supporting an unjust government in opposition to Communism; and so on.[10]

Lessons like these, if learned in time, would have helped to shape the methods of mission. The Church, alert to current needs, could then have adapted or discarded the old, inherited patterns wherever it became clear that they had ceased to express the Gospel for To-day. For it is not enough to be concerned with *techniques* of mission. In every place the Church has to learn to read the signs of the times, and to discern the uncriticized assumptions which militate against effective obedience to her Lord's command.

This is a hard and costly process. But if we can see ways in which a past generation of missionaries harmed their whole work, we may assume that our own efforts will be judged too, and that our faults will be equally obvious. Perhaps, in the light of the Bible and of the Holy Spirit's leading, these faults should be obvious already, while there is still time to put them right. There may not be much time.

If this principle of growth seems to imply belittlement of the pioneers of the Church's mission, let us state the simple truth: to stay alive means to change. In fact, pride in our heritage is a very good reason for wanting our work to be as relevant to our generation as the work of earlier missionaries was to theirs.

When we think of the pioneers, famous or unknown, who planted the Church in South Africa, we are filled with a humble admiration. Sometimes we are surprised to discover how up-to-date they seem in their desire to embody and express the Gospel. We think of the missionary of former days standing under a tree to preach, and so he did. But he did more. The Word of God did not go unsupported into the bush. "When the wagons rolled out of Capetown. . . . Robert had in the forechest his carpenter's and gardener's tools, a copy of *Young on Agriculture* and *Young on Botany,* a thermometer, a microscope, a pocket compass, some kitchen utensils, a fowling-piece, a Dutch grammar and dictionary. It was the standard missionary equipment, supplied to him for Africa as the key to husbandry, culture, and religion which nineteenth-century missions aimed at." The year was 1817 and the missionary was Robert Moffat.[11]

The aim of the missionaries was to see the Gospel which they preached take flesh, for they knew that a love that cares will never treat a man as though he were just a soul with ears. This caring love will make gardens in the desert, and build churches, schools, and hospitals, that men may know their whole life belongs to God.

All this has been done. But if the pioneers could come back to us, they would not tell us to live in the past, or to be satisfied with the present. They would tell us that we, too, must be pioneers.

The classic pattern of a mission station shows how the ministry of incarnation and identification worked out in practice. Church, school, and hospital stand grouped together; for spirit, mind, and body are all involved as

Christian workers seek to meet the need of the whole man in the whole situation.

The Church's concern for education and for the ministry of healing goes far back in history. In Western Europe the old patterns have been changing more and more as the state takes over activities that the Church began. Social welfare of many kinds is now accepted as a responsibility of the community. This is not necessarily a sinister development; it may be a sign that the conscience of a nation has been stirred to action. In principle at least, the Welfare State is a triumph for those who showed the way.

In South Africa the Church's medical work enjoys state support and continues alongside the official medical services. But in education the pattern has been drastically altered by the state's assertion of control over African schools through the Bantu Affairs Department. The Church's resistance to this was based not on conservatism, but on the knowledge that far from seeking to give African children opportunities to match their abilities, the state would set deliberate limitations to their development in the interests of a false ideology of blood and race. Statistics for the Matriculation Examination show how the standard of education has, in fact, deteriorated under state control.[12]

It is no use wishing that things were not so. Whatever may still be done through residential hostels for African school-children, the schools themselves have gone. But there are two ways of reacting to this fact. One is to cling to the mutilated pattern that remains, drawing in defensively like a beleaguered garrison that has lost one of its outposts. The other is to pursue a ministry of incarnation and identification *by whatever methods the present situation demands.*

Is our aim simply to cling to what we have? If so, the garrison may find that it is fighting a war that ended long ago, and our well-established mission stations may become massive irrelevancies.

It may be that the concept of mission as outgoing activity has been endangered by the very desire—however good and necessary—to express the Gospel through institutions. A great church may symbolize nobility, but not mobility. A hospital may serve thousands of patients, but red-blanketed heathen may be living on the opposite hill, and the only religious groups in the area that can show a growing membership may be separatist sects that are frankly racialist and only marginally Christian. Heroic efforts have to be made to keep church and hospital going and to serve out-stations and clinics with inadequate staff. Yet this does not make methods into ends. We have to ask, humbly but insistently, whether the ministry of evangelism is being crowded out.

NOTES

1. Hendrik Kraemer, *A Theology of the Laity*, p. 27.
2. Ibid., p. 28.
3. Ibid., p. 30.
4. *Missionary Commitments of the Anglican Communion*, p. 3.
5. Ibid., p. 18.
6. Brian Page, *The Harvest of Good Hope*, p. 5ff.
7. Ibid., p. 137.
8. *The Moving Spirit*, p. 86.
9. *Towards the Conversion of England*, p. 1.
10. *China: An Object Lesson*, E.H.P., p. 20ff.
11. I owe this point to a review, by Lawrence Benedict, of *Robert Moffatt, Pioneer in Africa,* by Cecil Northcott. The quotation is taken from the book, p. 39.

12.

	African matriculation candidates	Obtained matriculation exemption	Obtained school leaving certificate	Total percentage passes
1953	547	90	169	47.3
1954	523	127	107	44.7
1955	595	110	120	38.7
1956	768	164	190	46.1
1957	745	135	157	39.2
1958	660	113	153	37.6
1959	629	43	75	18.8
1960	716	28	100	17.9

For an interpretation of these figures, see *A Survey of Race Relations in South Africa*, 1961, South African Institute of Race Relations, p. 234-5.

3

Social Witness in South Africa

IF WE are seeking to give flesh to the Gospel, and to identify ourselves with the people of South Africa in general and the African people in particular, it may be that the really fundamental method to-day is not institutional at all. In the struggle for freedom and self-development, in the sheer battle to bring bread to the hungry, the African people do not look first of all for palliatives, but for other people to share the struggle with them. Hundreds of children suffering from malnutrition and tuberculosis are cared for in mission hospitals by doctors and nurses inspired by a sense of Christian vocation. This is a work which it would be impertinent to praise and indefensible to blame. Yet the Church will be judged by what she did to change the social order that made malnutrition and tuberculosis not only possible but prevalent.

At the New Delhi Assembly of the W.C.C., Mr Gabriel Setiloane said that the Churches would fail in South Africa unless they worked harder for the liberation of the African people. "Frustration and despair rule among my people," he said. "They are driven almost to the point where they are cursing God." A Southern Rhodesian delegate warned the Assembly that there was a danger that the Church would no longer appeal to young African intellectuals unless it took a stand in those areas where human dignity was not respected.[1] These are very moderate

19

expressions of a judgement that is widely made, more often in terms of repudiation of the Church than in terms of appeal to her.

Is such a judgement justified? The underlying question here is whether the Church has a message only for the individual, or whether it must bear witness also to society as a whole. That question should not be difficult for Anglicans to answer. Archbishop Clayton remarked in his charge to Provincial Synod in 1950: "I refuse as a Bishop in Christ's Holy Catholic Church to accept the position that the concern of the Church is only about the relation of an individual man with his God." We honour a particular line of social prophets, from F. D. Maurice to William Temple, in a long tradition of witness that goes back to the great Hebrew prophets of the eighth century before Christ. Our Lord himself introduced his mission with the words: "The Spirit of the Lord is upon me, because he has anointed me to preach good news to the poor. He has sent me to proclaim release to the captives, and recovering of sight to the blind, to set at liberty those who are oppressed, to proclaim the acceptable year of the Lord." (Luke 4. 18, 19.) Christ identified himself with the deprived and the oppressed: so must we.

In the light of Christ's incarnation and ministry, individualism is seen to be a distortion of the Gospel. All human life is intra-personal. We are persons-in-the-making, and it is through our relationships with other persons that we become persons. To be a Christian is to be committed to Christ and to one's fellow-men, and these two commitments go together. This truth is being realized afresh in an age when community relationships pose great problems for society. Class, race, colour: these groupings must cease to divide us if life is to be bearable. The world must become a neighbourhood if humanity is to survive.

So it is that the application and embodiment of salvation are sought to-day not in isolated individualism, but in reconciled community relationships. "Salvation . . . is concerned with men where they are, and does not seek to detach them from the world into pietistic groups." [2] The words of St Augustine, "Thou hast made us for thyself, and our hearts are restless till they find their rest in thee," have been changed by a later theologian to read, "Thou hast made us for thyself and for one another, and our hearts are restless until they find rest in thee in one another and in one another in thee." [3] The new phrase does not trip so glibly from the tongue, but it may be none the less true for that.

Christians are not sent out into the world to deal with selected aspects of human personality. They are there to make men whole. We do not preach at starving men; we try to show Christ's love by feeding them. What, then, must we do when men are hungry for the means of life—when they are oppressed by an unjust social order?

John Taylor begins his book, *Christianity and Politics in Africa,* with these words, "To-day it is not possible to live in Africa and to be indifferent to political questions." He goes on to make the claim : "A Church which was strong in faith and wisdom could speak to-day, as she has some-times spoken in other places and at other times, a prophetic word to make clear the way of justice and tolerance and human dignity. She could hold before men's eyes the values of the spirit, saving them from the false choices of material-ism and the false claims of the totalitarian way." The alternative is clear : "If the Church in Africa . . . gives the impression that God is not concerned with man's social and political affairs, then men will not be very much concerned with such a God. And this is not because men wish to use God for their own ends and demand that his thoughts shall be their thoughts; but if they feel that God cares nothing for the things which vitally affect their daily lives and stir their deepest emotions, they will not easily be persuaded that such a God loves them in any real sense at all." [4]

A vigorous and uncompromising social witness is called for. We must declare that South Africa's racial structure of society is incompatible with Christian values. But pronouncements are not enough; the social order must be changed.

This is the appeal of some of the outstanding African Christians to-day. They point out that "White South Africa" is doing a good deal to discredit in African eyes the Christianity which many of its members profess. This is the State that calls itself Christian. Many white citizens, who also call themselves Christian, stand aloof from the struggle for social justice. But surely, just *because* we are Christians, our calling is to get into the thick of the struggle, taking our Christianity with us. The Church must demonstrate the *relevance* of Christianity in the South African context, and this she has not always done. She has spoken up for principles, but principles remain disembodied until they are translated into practical concern for persons.

Ezekiel Mphahlele tells the story of a life restricted and oppressed, overshadowed by an inescapable sadness, the life of an urban African. He writes : "I tossed and turned in my waking and sleeping hours, and I saw no way out of the mental and spiritual conflicts that were harassing me. In 1947 I decided not to go to church any more. The white press, the white radio, the white Parliament, the white employers, the white Church babbled their platitudes and their lies about 'Christian trusteeship', the 'native emerging from primitive barbarism,' 'evangelizing the native', 'white guardianship'. Secular institutions wrenched the pulpit from the Church and cited the Scriptures, and the white man saw himself as an eternal missionary among non-whites. The Church raised an occasional feeble voice of protest. The non-white had for years been taught to love his neighbour—the white man; the non-European preacher, the non-European congregations, had taken refuge in the hope of eternal life. While the white preachers, through sermons broadcast over the radio, told their contented suburban congregations the story of Calvary and individual salvation, white churchgoers felt committed to group attitudes and the maintenance of mythical white supremacy. Equally, the white preacher felt committed to an ethic he did not dare apply to the necessity of group action against the forces of evil in a setting where such forces have worked themselves up into a savage national attitude said to be based on a Christian sense of justice." [5]

Again, and as a sober summing-up of an attitude painfully forced upon him by the crazy logic of South African life, Ezekiel Mphahlele writes : "The Church as an ecumenical force in South Africa has been on the retreat since before Union in 1910. And then the Church, with its emphasis on the value of the individual personality, has continued stubbornly to bring outmoded standards to the situation; a situation where a powerful *herrenvolk* has for three centuries done everything in the interests of the *volk*.

Where persons have been oppressed as a race group, the Church has sought safeguards and concessions for the individual, evading the necessity and responsibility of group action. And while it fixed its gaze on Calvary or kept up an

aloofness from political realities, the road has been slipping
back under its feet. It never seems to have occurred to the
Church that right under its nose has been growing a cal-
culating white barbarism, among those it considered as
hereditary custodians of Christianity, custodians who need
mission stations in their very midst. I cannot but reaffirm
what I said in a B.B.C. talk in 1955 on the African intellectual : that to us, the Church has become a symbol of the
dishonesty of the West." [6]

The man who writes these words used to be an Anglican.
So we find ourselves under scrutiny and criticism from
fellow-Christians, and former Christians, who cannot take
seriously our denunciation of communists and our disagree-
ment with Muslims as long as we ourselves remain outside
the conflict. They judge the sincerity of our views by the
effects they have in our own lives.

We do, of course, criticize communism. We know that it
is not the answer to South Africa's need. But do we exert
ourselves to present the *Christian* answer? We deplore
a society which bans the communist—and incidentally
defines communism in such general terms that the smear can
be extended conveniently to cover any critic—while all the
time it is using the very weapons of communism itself, fear
and force. We find it tragic that South Africa maintains
precisely those conditions in which communism can flourish,
conditions of sustained deprivation that make even des-
perate remedies attractive. But what are we doing to change
this permanent, underlying state of things? So, too, we
regret the appearance of the fez in the urban African town-
ships, yet we have to admit that the Christian brotherhood
we can offer is often conditioned by the "South African way
of life". It has not got beyond race. It may be multi-racial,
but it is not yet non-racial. If it is really superior to the

brotherhood of Islam is should be able to speak for itself.

"By their fruits ye shall know them" : this is a Christian criterion, and it is very generally used by non-Christians also. Our attitude towards the dispossessed, the needy, and the powerless is under judgement. Africans do not fail to notice the gap between profession and action among white Christians. We may preach equality, but do we practise it? Many of the younger African leaders would go much further; for them, Christianity is consciously associated with white supremacy, it is seen as a form of oppression. It is no accident that African Christians are commonly suspect among their own people as sell-outs and quislings. We have to face the possibility that by our failure to show our love for our neighbours, by concern for their poverty and exclusion, we may be preventing people from reaching God —an attitude for which the severest condemnation is reserved in the Gospels.[7]

If we take the Gospel seriously, where does it lead us? First of all, it leads us beyond the point where we can put the blame for everything on the present Government of the Republic. Christians rightly declare their opposition to every evil and oppressive measure, but behind the spate of legislation lies a social order which the legislation is designed to maintain. This form of society is not a new thing. As an African put it, "Oppression cannot all be blamed on the Nats : it was there before." The chain of segregational legislation goes back at least as far as the Natives Land Act of 1913.[8] We are concerned not merely to bewail the symptoms, but to eradicate the disease.

Secondly, the Gospel carries us beyond the point where we imagine that poverty can be dealt with by acts of charity. This does not mean that we are to stop being interested in the voluntary relief of need, or to pull out of the social centres, the clubs and crèches, the clinics and the night-schools. It means that we cannot allow these activities to become a substitute for hard thinking about wages, production, and the distribution of wealth. What William Temple wrote of Britain in the nineteen forties is true of South Africa twenty years later : "The existing system is challenged on moral grounds. It is not merely that some who 'have not' are jealous of some who 'have'. The charge against our social system is one of injustice. The banner so familiar in earlier unemployed or socialist processions— 'Damn your charity; we want justice'— vividly exposes the situation as it was seen by its critics. If the present order is taken for granted or assumed to be sacrosanct, charity from the more to the less fortunate would seem virtuous and commendable; to those for whom the order itself is suspect or worse, such charity is blood-money. Why should some be in a position to dispense and others to need that kind of charity?" [9]

A very general rise in wages is necessary. In the peri-urban areas of Cape Town, for example, the proportion of Africans living below the Poverty Datum Line is between fifty and eighty per cent. This is a situation that cannot be dealt with by the isolated acts of individuals. Every employer has a moral duty to pay a fair wage, but the mere pushing up of wages here and there tends to cause an increase in unemployment as the labour force is pruned and competition is intensified. The widespread change that is needed will have to be linked to an expanding economy and rising production. We need a redistribution of wealth, and the economic process must be geared to this end.

The present restrictions imposed upon the non-white people of South Africa through Job Reservation and prohibitions limiting the acquirement of technical skills can be justified only if race is accepted as an ultimate value. But such an assumption is indefensible on any Christian basis. Again and again Anglicans have been quite explicit in condemning discrimination between people on grounds of race alone. As a logical inference from this principle, the Lambeth Conference of 1958 included the following paragraph in its Resolutions :

"The Conference would urge that in multi-racial societies members of all races should be allowed :

(a) a fair and just share in the government of their country;

(b) a fair and just share in the control, development, and rewards of the natural resources of their country, including advancement to the highest level of attainment;

(c) the right to associate freely in worship, in education, in industry, in recreation, and in all other departments of the common life." [10]

How can Christians accept the uprooting of families and communities to maintain racial separation under the Group Areas legislation? How can we support a system of migratory labour which involves the long-term separation of families? Such inhumane laws cannot be humanely administered. They must be repealed. If we could identify ourselves with the other man, and experience even in imagination the pain and humiliation of his daily life, we should not condone the maintenance of the present order for a moment longer. Our social complacency is only made possible by this failure to cross to the other side in sympathy and understanding. To-day the Africans are saying that the white man will have to suffer himself—not in imagination but in fact— before there can be understanding, or even negotiation, between black and white. Only the common experience of suffering will produce a common language.

What is it that seals us off from this suffering now? Lack of contact breeds ignorance, and ignorance breeds complacency, if not prejudice. In the end we do not want to know the truth. And then there is the fact that our ordered, institutional life as a missionary Church keeps us fully occupied. *Institutionalism makes for conservatism.* The suggestion that it may be better to keep quiet and do what good you can is subtly persuasive. As Dietrich Bonhoeffer realized, even a missionary purpose can lead to a deliberate conformity to the world, and this conformity may be a bushel which puts out the Christian light.[11] This is the answer to those who suggest that to enter the social and political struggle is to invite attack by the powers that be, and that this will mean the loss of hard-won opportunities for witness and service.

There is no doubt that in South Africa to-day a Church whose social witness is uncompromising will stand in jeopardy. Yet we are called to be precisely a Church like that. "A religion which is not related positively to the total developing life of the community will never do for Africa. But neither will a social gospel busily engaged in a programme of improvement which leaves the deep personal levels of human nature untransformed. The heart of the matter is the urgent need for a Church in Africa which is both supernatural and responsible in the full meaning of both those words." [12]

We may find ourselves under fire from both sides, attacked by the rival nationalisms, white and black. We cannot identify ourselves with either side, for the false premise of racial domination is accepted by the extremists of both. In such a situation we are called to be a Confessing

Church, like the Church in Germany under the Nazis. When the question, "If we take the Gospel seriously, where does it lead us?" was put to a group of young people at a missionary conference in Cape Town, they replied, "To the gallows." The Chairman's comment was, "Well, it took Christ there." A Confessing Church in South Africa will certainly suffer. This is our vocation.

We affirm our belief in the natural dignity and value of every man, of whatever colour or race, as created in the image of God.[13] And this belief leads us to claim for every man the means to live a good life. The freedom of the person under the rule of law is a necessary Christian concern. "Christianity taught us care," said von Hügel, "Caring matters most." Christianity did not teach us to care for disembodied souls, or for isolated individuals, but for persons in society.

Effective mission demands a genuine interest in the whole life of the people to whom the missionary is sent. "As long as a man feels that he is the object of interest only for reasons of intellectual curiosity or for purposes of conversion, and not because of himself as he is in his total empirical reality, there cannot arise that humane, natural contact which is the indispensable condition of all real religious meeting of man with man."[14] Without such real concern, the ameliorative work of Christian missions will seem like offering a hearty breakfast to the man in the condemned cell.

NOTES

1. Report in *The Church Times,* 24 November, 1961.
2. Minute of the Provincial Board of Missionary Strategy, 22 February, 1962.
3. H. H. Farmer, *The Servant of the Word,* p. 39, quoted by Reuel L. Howe in *Man's Need and God's Action,* p. 11.
4. J. V. Taylor, *Christianity and Politics in Africa,* p. 7-9.
5. Ezekiel Mphahlele, *Down Second Avenue,* p. 163.
6. Ibid., p. 221.
7. In this and the following section, as in much else, I am indebted to Professor Monica Wilson.
8. See Bengt Sundkler, *Bantu Prophets in South Africa,* p. 33.
9. William Temple, *Christianity and Social Order,* p. 14.
10. Resolution 110, *The Lambeth Conference, 1958,* p. 1.56.
11. Dietrich Bonhoeffer, *The Cost of Discipleship,* p. 106.
12. J. V. Taylor, *Christianity and Politics in Africa,* p. 20.
13. Resolution 110, *The Lambeth Conference, 1958,* p. 1. 55-56.
14. Hendrik Kraemer, *The Christian Message in a Non-Christian World,* p. 140.

4

The end of Paternalism

CHRISTIAN missionaries in many parts of Africa have come to a painful awareness that the Christianity presented to Africa by Western men has been a Christianity in Western dress, and that this is ultimately resented. Christ, after all, never visited Europe, but he was a refugee in Africa as a child. To-day Christians are trying to discern and to separrate what is Western, what is African, and what is Christian. It would not be unfair to generalize from their conclusions, and to summarize what many of them would now admit : that our Christianity has been too individualistic, too philosophical, too organizational, too ready to pull down the pillars of African custom. It has been too much the religion of the white man, and yet too little practised by him. The searing remark of an African shows that this rethinking is no merely academic exercise : "If this religion was that good, do you think that its originators—the whites—would have abandoned it?"

It is not that we want to blunt the cutting edge of the Christian Gospel by syncretism and assimilation : in fact, our weakness has been precisely in allowing the Gospel to become too closely associated with the transient secular patterns of Western life—there has been too much syncretism and assimilation already.

The rapid and widespread growth of Zionist sects, unconnected with any of the great historical Christian traditions, is a sign that the situation cannot be left to sort itself out. No doubt Zionism has many causes. Resentment of discipline in the historic Churches often leads to a split. But this may be the match which touches off the explosion rather than the gunpowder which explains its size. It is the reaction of Africans to the colour bar, and to the generally Westernized form of the traditional Churches, that explains the attraction of the separatist sects.

When the Church denies some fundamental principle of its own being, as it does when it tolerates discrimination on grounds of race alone, then a movement which might have been a genuine revival becomes a separatist protest against such a Church. For all our efforts towards integration, the Church still appears to be equivocal on the subject of colour. Max Warren comments, "It is impossible to condemn the African for being separatist when he is treated as a separate person." He adds, "The fact that in addition to being separated within the Church he was subordinated as well, and so was unable to exercise either initiative or authority, powerfully conduced to the act of formal separation. . . . Separation was a protest that the Church needed to be reformed at a decisive point in its life, the point where its transcendent unity was denied by the intrusion of a colour bar." [1]

The desire and need for community; the desire and need for an indigenous expression of Christian worship; the frustrated capacity for leadership and the longing for a rebirth of African greatness and independence : all these contribute to the growth of Zionism. Then there is the central place of healing among the Zionists. It is not that we have altogether neglected this ministry of healing. But in our mission hospitals there has sometimes been an apparent separation between the Church's life of prayer and her healing work through scientific diagnosis and treatment. In Zionism everything is more personal and more immediate. Sundkler's comment seems significant: "A mission doctor who used to call nurses, patient, and relatives together for prayer before performing an operation was often referred to by Zionists as a real Christian in whom they had confidence." [2]

The fault on the part of Western missionaries and white Church-members can be summed up in the word "paternalism". It is the attitude of "father knows best" that provokes the deepest resentment. In circumstances like these, says Roland Allen, if a prophet arose he would either have all the spirit crushed out of him, or he would secede.[3] These things have happened all too often. That they need not happen is illustrated by a missionary in the Transkei, who writes of the work of a Coloured Churchwoman there who has a real gift of healing and evangelism. "She had a serious illness about ten years ago during which she had a vision in which she was commissioned to work and to heal. One of the good things about her is the way in which her own Church life is developing; and another is the way in which she seems able to meet the condition of primitive heathen people and of many who have lapsed from the Church to become witch doctors. Our Church congregations in certain districts have grown very much through her work." The missionary adds: "Another thing which we have been doing for many years is each quarter, to send a group of lay preachers to one district to stay for three days and pray and preach and visit the heathen and the lapsed. But the backbone of witness everywhere, I am convinced, must be the persevering everyday contacts of the faithful and the witness of the regular life and worship of the Church."

Surely, then, paternalism is a dead horse to-day? If so, one can only comment that a dead horse can spread a great deal of infection. It is flattering to think that paternalism came to an end with the Victorian era, but unfortunately it is not true. In fact, Africans have often commented on the exclusiveness of the later missionaries as compared with the earlier ones : "When we went to see him he kept us waiting, and then came out of the house to us—he would not ask us in." The missionary of earlier days was more likely to live in close relationship with his people, even if he did regard them as *his* people.

Of that older paternalism, as John Taylor points out, it can at least be said that it was a form of love. Its fault was that it was a protective and possessive love—a love that refused to take risks with the Church. The Western missionaries saw themselves as the teachers, counsellors, directors, and leaders of the people. And the idea caught on : "The principle of tutelage was projected into the African Church itself. Its presence is betrayed in the fact that the work of its leaders became more and more supervisory in emphasis, and the Church itself began to resemble a bureaucracy in which every official has to be answerable to the man above him." [4] The new paternalism tends to be as authoritarian as the old, but perhaps less intimate and less loving.

Is our aloofness the sign of something else—of our desire to be respected, and to be respectable? Is it, perhaps, the fruit of pride, of the love of authority, of the tendency to cling to power? Is it that we want to keep our distance, to do good to people and to be appropriately thanked for doing it? It is very natural that we should desire appreciation. It is not, however, very supernatural. Dr Anthony Barker writes : "It is a great weakness in us that we seek reassurance for ourselves in asking gratitude from those we are

34

privileged to help. St Vincent de Paul used to advise his flock of devoted workers : 'When you go out to do good to the poor, beg them to forgive you,' and so reminds us how hard it is to receive benefits at the hands of another." [5]

All who are called to Christian ministry, in whatever capacity, need to come back again and again to the "forgotten sacrament" of the feet-washing, where the Christ who said "I am among you as he that serveth" gave a deliberate object-lesson to his followers. *This* is what our ministry is to be like.

The dangers of paternalism were well expressed by Roland Allen fifty years ago : "A tradition very rapidly grows up that nothing can be done without the authority and guidance of the missionary, the people wait for him to move, and the longer they do so, the more incapable they become of any independent action. Thus the leader is confirmed in the habit of gathering all authority into his own hands, and of despising the powers of his people, until he makes their inactivity an excuse for denying their capacity." [6]

Is there, however, a legitimate and *necessary* form of paternalism—a wise leadership and firm guidance shorn of pride and privilege? The Reverend Arthur Lewis, writing of a primitive mission-district in Rhodesia, says frankly that in such a place "if the Church were not paternalist it would perish". He adds : "But every missionary knows his vocation is to work himself out of a job, to share and hand over responsibility as soon as he can." [7]

This is the dilemma. To hand over responsibility too soon would be irresponsible. Where Christians are weak and paganism is strong, where those who shout loudest are least willing to bear the cost of leadership, it may be that the easy way out is not the right way. Abdication is easy. So is the imposition of an authoritarian regime. But the right way is a partnership in which responsibility is shared and through which leadership is developed.

Withdrawal of some kind may be necessary, but John Taylor has shown how easily withdrawal can go wrong—it can be "withdrawal upwards" instead of "withdrawal sideways". Writing of the Church in Buganda, he says: "Missionaries were committed to a policy of handing over responsibility into African hands, but the Church structure enabled them to do so always by withdrawing upwards into a higher level in the administrative hierarchy, instead of withdrawing sideways so as to make room for African colleagues working beside them as fellow-members of the same category. But it was even more serious when the movement of withdrawal upwards 'caught on,' as when a spoon is lifted from a tin of treacle." [8]

The process of development from paternalism to partnership, and ultimately to withdrawal of the Western missionaries, is so widespread to-day that we need to ask whether there are any special factors in the South African situation which make it hazardous to draw inferences from other and different situations. There is much common ground. A missionary in the diocese of St John's writes: "We are generally feeling in this diocese that there has to be a wholesale change of the traditional techniques by which the missionary activity was launched here. They have to some extent brought us to the stage at which we think we can see the missionary activity becoming a Church: and now new methods must be used to cope with the whole range of problems associated with 'letting the Church be—or become —the Church'." This would be true of many other territories. But there is one great difference. In those areas, generally speaking, the Christian mission is being carried out in societies which have developed from colonial rule to independence. In South Africa the Government envisages separate development, but certainly not the abdication of power by the white minority. And while the Church opposes this concept of parallel but separate development, as incompatible with Christian community and with the life of a modern industrial state, it holds that people of different racial groups—black and white, Coloured and Asiatic—all belong in South Africa and all belong *together*.

Here in the Republic we have a great opportunity to show what it means that Christ has identified himself with *humanity* by becoming Man : to demonstrate that as Christians our solidarity is with *humanity,* not with a group defined in terms of colour, language, nationality, or culture. Our situation is different from that of the Philippine Episcopal Church, for example, whose missionary bishop writes : "Foreign and professional missionaries, charged with the initial responsibility of leadership, must so order their lives, attitudes, and outlook that they increasingly move from doing things for the younger Church or the members of the young Church to doing things with and in the young Church; and eventually, by God's grace, work themselves out of their positions." [9] Few missionaries in South Africa are "foreign" in this sense, whatever their ethnic origins. As the Church grows, they may well have a different part to play in its total life. A good deal of "withdrawal sideways" may be necessary. But the aim is not a mono-racial Church. The aim goes beyond patronage, beyond paternalism, beyond parallelism, even beyond partnership. The aim is a *non-racial* Church, a Church in which race is simply irrelevant, except in so far as it may contribute to a richer harmony.

This last point may be important. When St Paul wrote, in Galatians 3. 28, "Gone is the distinction between Jew and Greek, slave and free man, male and female—you are all one in Christ Jesus," the inference is not that differences *disappeared,* but that they *ceased to divide.* The inclusion of "male and female" in the list shows that. Children were still boys or girls, and not mixed infants. Men and women were not replaced by hermaphrodites. But the difference of sex became the potential of a richer harmony—it was redeemed.

So, too, there would be no advance in the attempt to reduce our varied riches of culture and background to a common mediocrity. That would be retrogression. What we look for and long for is a Church in which black and white belong together, a Church in which race has ceased to be a criterion, a Church which holds in its one corporate life *all* the riches of our wide heritage.

It is this quality of community that has to be demonstrated now, at the local level, in every parish of the Province. Our calling is a difficult one : to make an institutional religion come alive in a revolutionary situation. The answer, surely, is that it is *the Church* that must be revolutionary. She cannot be a calming and stabilizing factor : sin cannot be condoned. "The Church is called to the task of ferment and upheaval in humanity attacking the stabilization of orders fashioned to suit human selfishness." [10] As Alan Paton put it, when speaking at the All-Africa Churches' Conference at Ibadan in 1958, "Our churches are to a dangerous degree conforming churches. and instead of transforming society have become conformed to it . . . The people of Africa are on the march into the modern age; and the Church must march with them, the guardian not of what is old but of what is ageless." [11]

The sin of worldliness among Christians has often been defined in terms of personal pleasures and indulgences; it could more aptly be defined in terms of acquiescence in the world's oppression of persons through corrupt social orders. Could anyone be more worldly than the man who does not drink, smoke, swear, dance, or go to the theatre, and yet who remains passive in the face of social evil? As Dietrich Bonhoeffer understood, we need a holy worldliness or a worldly holiness—a Christian faith and practice both relevant and revolutionary.

Christians are often deterred from taking the very first steps along this path by an embarrassment that arises because these simple steps are considered unusual or unacceptable by others. Are we to do only what the world considers customary? Inter-racial meeting and mixing is found to be "artificial", and therefore it is not pursued. Is it not the fact that it is the so-called "South African way of life" that is artificial? To treat people as people is more natural, and also more Christian, than to treat them as representatives of a race or class or group.

We need the courage to allow Christian community to come alive, whatever the neighbours may say. For what matters about our Christian institutions is not simply the good work they do, but the quality of corporate life they demonstrate. "The Church is to express in its corporate life the nature and the quality of God's redeeming work." [12] This life is, in fact, itself a method of mission, and a very important one.

The story of Florence Allshorn's experience as a young missionary in Uganda is a powerful illustration of this truth. "Seven young missionaries had been sent to the

39

4

Iganga station in as many years, and none had been willing to stay. The difficulty was not only the debilitating and nerve-racking effect of the climate, but also the temperament of the senior woman missionary. She was of the pioneer type and very wiry. She had quelled single-handed attacks of plague by burning down whole villages, and she ruled her kingdom with an arm of steel. She gave herself to the people and expected others to do the same. She was impervious to the newer ideas about missionary work that were stirring in the minds of younger missionaries. She had come out to save the souls of the heathen, and save them she would, even if it meant pursuing a malefactor round and round the table with a stick, or that no one had been able in past years to live with her. When Florence arrived she found the one and only sitting-room divided into two halves. In the one was cramped together all the senior's furniture; the other half was entirely bare. 'That's your half,' she was informed." [13]

How to live together : this was the problem. And it was not a problem beyond and apart from the work of witness— it was inseparably bound up with it. One day the African Matron said to her : "I have been on this station for fifteen years and I have seen you come out, all of you saying you have brought to us a Saviour, but I have never seen this situation saved yet." [14] Here was a situation that had to be redeemed if mission was to become effective. The redemption of personal relationships, whether or not they involve differences of race, is essential wherever we preach Christ. In such redeemed relationships paternalism (or maternalism) dies. The old possessive love or the new authoritarian temper cannot live in the presence of him who said, "Don't you ever be called 'rabbi'—you have only one teacher, and all of you are brothers. And don't call any human being 'father'—for you have one Father and he is in Heaven. And you must not let people call you 'leaders'— you have only one leader, Christ! The only 'superior' among you is the one who serves the others. For every man who promotes himself will be humbled, and every man who learns to be humble will find promotion." [15]

NOTES

1. Max Warren in *Revival*. This conclusion is supported by Dr Sundkler, and Dr Edgar Brookes takes the same view: "Separation has been the result, to a very large extent, of the presence of the colour bar within the Christian Church." (Edgar Brookes, *A Century of Missions in Natal and Zululand*, p. 32.)
2. Bengt Sundkler, *Bantu Prophets in South Africa*, p. 237.
3. Roland Allen, *Missionary Methods: St Paul's or Ours?* p. 106.
4. J. V. Taylor, *Processes of Growth in an African Church*, p. 12-13.
5. Anthony Barker in *Compassion,* No. 2, 1962.
6. Op. cit., p. 105.
7. Arthur Lewis, "Winds of Change in an African Valley", *The Church Times*, 6 April, 1962.
8. J. V. Taylor, *Processes of Growth in an African Church*, p. 14.
9. The Right Reverend Lyman C. Ogilby, in *Viewpoints*, p. 251.
10. T. F. Torrance, *Conflict and Agreement in the Church,* Vol. 1, p. 224. On a wider scale, this was the message of the Whitby meeting of the Committee of the International Missionary Council in 1947. Coming together under the title, "Christian Witness in a Revolutionary World", the Committee issued its statements under the heading, *The Witness of a Revolutionary Church.*

11. *The Church in Changing Africa*, p. 54.
12. J. A. T. Robinson in *The Historic Episcopate*.
13. J. H. Oldham, *Florence Allshorn*, p. 23.
14. Ibid., p. 28.
15. Matthew 23, 8-12.

5

Mission to the Heathen

WHEN the map of Africa is divided into areas where different religions predominate, it is a sobering sight for Christians. To the North, Islam is virtually in control, with perhaps eighty million adherents in Africa as a whole. The great central mass of the continent, from a line across its widest point down to a line joining Angola and Mozambique, is perhaps best described as "animist", though this convenient term is too simple to be wholly true. Geoffrey Parrinder writes : "It cannot be said that Africans are simply animists, believing in personal spirits and polytheistic pantheons. Nor are they merely anamatists, thinking of unco-ordinated energies. A few writers would even call them monotheists, since all powers are subject to the Supreme Being. But this again would over-simplify the picture. The fact is that we find mixed types of religious belief, in which different phases are found side by side : dynamism, spiritism, and theism." [1]

There may be as many as a hundred million followers of African traditional religions in the whole continent. There are only about thirty-two million Christians.[2] This, in itself, is disturbing, and so is the extent to which Christianity has remained in the coastal areas where it was brought by Western missionaries. The Coptic and Ethiopian Churches are exceptions. So, also, is Uganda, which although it is far inland and only received its first missionaries in

1877, is a Christian country—statistically the most Christian on the whole continent.

When we come down to South Africa, which is so often regarded by its white citizens as a bastion of the Faith, we find that after three hundred years of white settlement a third of the African population is not even nominally Christian. Three and a half million people out of South Africa's total of 15,841,128 of all races are officially classed as having no affiliation to any Christian body.[3] The great majority of these people are African traditionalists, those who still stand by the indigenous way of life, including pagan religion. Among the Xhosa they are know as *abantu ababomvu*—Red People, from the ochre-dyed blankets and mud-smeared faces which provide local colour for the cameras of tourists on the Garden Route. But, as Philip Mayer says, " 'Red' Xhosa are not just a few picturesque survivals : on the contrary, they are a flourishing half of the Xhosa people to-day, and are particularly strong in the areas nearest to East London." [4]

Those three hundred years of white settlement in South Africa do not mean that there have been three hundred years of missionary advance. As late as 1823, William Shaw could look north from his field of work in Kaffraria and say, "There is not a single missionary station between the place of my residence and the northern extremity of the Red Sea." But even a hundred and forty years is a long time, as the Church's mission in Africa is measured. East London is a long-established civic community. Yet in this very area eighty-five per cent of the Xhosa peasant population is still pagan.[5]

It is not only in the Transkei and the Ciskei that the Church is in contact with the heathen. The same mission goes on in Zululand and Swaziland, Ovamboland and

Vendaland, Basutoland and Lebombo. To South African Christians these facts present an inescapable challenge. Whatever new approaches we make to the problems of the Church's mission, we dare not and cannot ignore Christ's command to preach the Gospel—to confront the heathen with his claim and to bring them into his Church. This is our primary responsibility, and therefore these people—the heathen in our midst—are our responsibility too.

It is possible to distinguish a number of different fields in which the Church seems to be immobilized or on the defensive in its work among Africans. There are politically-conscious Africans who are leaving us because the actions and attitudes of white people do not commend Christianity to them. Many of these African intellectuals owe their early training to mission schools, and their repudiation of the Christian faith, as we have seen, has not necessarily been a shallow or easy thing.

Secondly, there are serious losses to "Ethiopian", Zionist, and Messianic sects which have accommodated themselves to the psychology and the aspirations of dispossessed African people, and which are heretical as well as schismatic. And, thirdly, there is the still unevangelized mass of the "Red People," who for a hundred and forty years have been looking askance both at the white people and at their fellow-tribesmen who have embraced the Christian religion and much of the Western way of life. They are the hard core of heathenism, and their conversion is made all the more difficult by the fact that for generations they have been living side by side with Christians of varying degrees of conscientiousness.

It would probably be an over-simplification to differentiate too sharply between these three areas of challenge to the Church. A politically-conscious African nationalism and a self-conscious "Africanism"—the search for an African personality and identity—may seem poles apart from the conservatism of traditional religion maintaining itself despite all the pressures of secular society. But in fact there is a vast area in which the old and the new are mixed, with infinite variations on the themes of resentment and reaction, radicalism and conservatism, freedom and tradition. Sophisticated chiefs and simple peasants may both be found moving towards the cult of a Black Messiah, no doubt for different reasons. Fr Tempels may be right when he asserts that African paganism aspires from the root of its soul towards the very soul of Christian spirituality, but what if Christian spirituality seems inseparably connected with white domination and the notice "Net vir blankes"? Christians believe that Christ has fulfilled all man's restless longings and hopes for a God who cares, but the "White Christ" is not recognized as meeting this need, except for the whites.

The resistance of pagan Africans to the Christian appeal is not hard to understand, though it cannot excuse us from our responsibility. What is harder to face, and all the more necessary to face because it is in our own control, is our lack of persistence in making the appeal, the falling-off of impetus in our missionary advance, and our tendency to be content with a settled, institutional Christian life. Yet these are the facts as reported by missionaries, and this is their assessment: *the old techniques of mission have become outmoded, but generally speaking they have not yet been replaced.*

Foremost among the Church's converting agencies were the schools which she established throughout the length and breadth of Africa. The Reverend Cyprian Thorpe writes of these mission schools: "To the missionary they were often a headache and a heart-ache, but none can deny the converting potential which they represented. The teacher was often the outstation catechist; the children were taught the Scriptures in school and attended hearers' and catechumens' classes after school. Heathen parents were brought into contact with Christianity through the schools, and sometimes the children themselves would be the bearers of the Good News to their parents. Now, in the Republic at any rate, this potential has largely disappeared."

Fr Thorpe goes on : "Another powerful converting agency which is losing its edge is the voluntary catechist (or preacher, as he is called in some places) who, though often unlettered, by his preaching and living the Gospel brought many converts to the Faith. The demands of earning a living in a society which is based on a cash and not a pastoral economy have reduced both the numbers of men who can give their time to this work, and also the amount of time which those who are still available can devote to it."

"But the efficacy of the Church has not only suffered from outside causes. There has been an undoubted loss of evangelical zeal. As more and more people became Christians the tendency to associate with each other to the exclusion of non-Christians increased. There has been a tendency for the Church to over-institutionalize itself . . . Mayer shows conclusively that there has been a hardening of social patterns as between Red (heathen) and School (Christian) groups. The longer we wait the harder it will become to bridge the gap and to make converts."

Here is a clear call to the Church of the Province as a whole, to provide the men and supply the money to take the Gospel of Christ to the heathen, and to do it now.

There has been a good deal of heart-searching about the recent formation of a Provincial missionary association, the Society of Missionary Churchmen. In some ways it seemed a retrogressive step, perhaps suggesting a restricting of mission to one field when we want to see it implemented in every field. But here is a particular need which a Provincial missionary association will help to meet. It is not as though we could turn away from the old work of mission-to-the-heathen as something now completed. It is not completed—far from it. The old work must go on *in new ways,* and we are all called to take an active part in it by our prayers and gifts.

What are these "new ways"? The Reverend Alex King suggests, first, that rural work among Africans should be regarded as a specialist job. It involves particular problems of language, literacy, and communication, and we cannot assume that these problems are automatically solved by handing over more and more of this work to African priests. Urban Africans may be out of touch with the tribal life of the reserves. An African priest brought up in the Kimberley area confessed that his education had been entirely in English and Afrikaans and he could not speak Setswana. Whoever is doing this rural work, and whatever his race, special gifts and special training are called for, and it is suggested that the selection and training of men requires Province-wide co-operation. In all this "the language-factor is *quite* dominant : how can there be any communication unless the agents at work have such a mastery of the local language that they can make the initial break-through and maintain it? . . . On the reverse side is the need to ensure that all our workers—lay or priestly—are really fluent in reading English. With the paucity of vernacular literature it is essential that such people can make use of the material available for them in English."

New thinking is called for because the Church cannot stand outside the social and economic scheme of things, or remain unaffected by the Bantustan idea (however much she may dislike it), except at the cost of fostering an inward-turning pietism. She must not continue uncritically with old techniques of mission when the conditions of life are changing : her strategy must be relevant to the times and her concern for the whole of life must be clearly shown. "The Church must involve herself in a situation which is involving so many of her people," writes Fr King, ". . . I think it is only by becoming progressively involved in the situation that we can hope to cause the Church to develop towards a healthy idea of itself as the redeeming, outreaching organism it is."

In the country districts our present use of manpower is all based upon the idea of a peripatetic ordained ministry whose chief concern is to maintain the pastoral stability of the existing Church, largely through periodic administration of the sacraments. One of the weaknesses of this system is that people are taught to live a sacramental life which is then largely denied them, because the visits of the priest are necessarily few and far between. Another weakness is that the emphasis falls on maintenance rather than extension.

What we need, it is suggested, is that the priest should become primarily the *teacher* of the Church, that he should concentrate on lay-leadership training, and that this training should be closely related to the real situation of the rural Church to-day. In working out methods of training the group-system should be used, as something already inherent in African thought and life, and both the family-clan unit and sex-age grouping should be taken into account.

But how can all this be done without neglecting the administration of the sacraments, which occupies most of the priest's time during his monthly visit to an outstation? The answer may seem startling, but because it comes from missionaries who speak from within the situation and with direct experience of its problems it deserves humble and careful consideration. It is that *there should be a large-scale extension of the part-time ordained ministry.*

This would mean that proved leaders of the local congregation would be admitted to priests' orders with a limited function of ministry. A teacher, for example, would remain in his employment, but out of school he would do the sacramental things needed by the local Church. He would celebrate the Holy Communion, baptize, visit and minister to the sick, hear confessions, and (under supervision) deal with disciplinary problems. Not only would this mean that the local Church could really base its life and activity and worship around the Eucharist, but it would set free the full-time ministry for a great development of instruction and evangelism. And instead of being a frontier-post, the outstation or village Church would be transformed into a vital centre of life and witness.

Fr King writes: "What I plead for now is a recognition of the importance of the outstation Church as being the major focal point of the Church's mission to the world, and an adjustment of strategy that will enable the whole resource of the Church to be poured into the transformation of the local outstation Church and congregation till they really do become in every place the worshipping, living, militant body they must become." The means to this end would be "a local part-time ministry to supply the sacramental basis on which alone that living local Church can be built up and nourished, and a full-time, professional, specialist ministry setting themselves to direct and mobilize that local Church to its onslaught on the world."

These suggestions are supported by the argument of Harris and Parrinder in *The Christian Approach to the Animist.* They see the need for missionaries to be set free from office work and administration so that they can spend time with the people and really understand their language and their customs. And they stress the importance of the sacramental life of the local Church : "The Animist is a member of a sacramental society. At his many praying-places he often takes part in ceremonies which involve a common meal and food shared with the spirits. It is pathetic to find that so often, when a man becomes a Christian and has renounced spirit-worship, he is only able to attend a service of Holy Communion two or three times a year. This is largely due to the shortage of ordained clergy and the large areas they have to cover. There is need for an adaptation of the system of clergy, and perhaps for part-time clergy who support themselves by manual work and so are in close touch with the people, like the worker-priests of France. The Animist has a genius for sacramental worship, and everything should be done to see that it finds its fullest expression in the Christian rite." Only a full-bodied Christianity will do for Africa : "For the Animist religion covers the whole of life, and part of the Christian approach is to demonstrate in practice that Christianity does so also."[6]

A change along these lines might mean that there would be a new and exciting rôle for the big mission-station, as the research and planning centre for a whole district. Perhaps even more exciting is the suggestion that we should

experiment with the infiltration of the "Red world"—
"training a priest and his family, plus one or two other
families, then putting them back into blankets and planting
them in a particular area on a special 'mission to the red'."
English pastoral techniques and Western individualism are
certainly less apposite to Africa than group-living, group-
witnessing, and identification with the local community.

Here, then, are some of the changes that may be called
for, or at least some of the suggestions that must be considered. But a deeper question is raised by this issue of the
heathen in our midst, and again it is a missionary who
poses it: "Have missionaries ever penetrated sufficiently
into the cultural and religious background of the peoples of
South Africa? Has there not been a failure to see in the
ancestor-cult and in the sacrificial customs of the Southern
Bantu an African 'Old Testament' which was making them
ready for the New?"

The traditional world-view of African people has not
been changed by city life, or by a life divided between the
urban locations and the rural reserves. In a general survey,
Geoffrey Parrinder points out that the unseen influence of
the ancestors, the fear of witches, and the power of the
witch-doctor (or witch-finder) have stood the strain of
removal to town life, and have even multiplied to meet new
circumstances. "Even in the towns, and among those who
have accepted the new religions, there is a great substratum
of traditional beliefs which must never be left out of
account in an assessment of religious life. The ancient ideas
constantly reappear in the separatist Christian sects, and in
the magical and witchcraft beliefs which most people still
hold."[7]

This is certainly true in South Africa. Many African

Christians, who have been led to a theoretical rejection of these traditional ideas, are in fact still strongly influenced by them. They would assume, at the very least, that to neglect the wishes of the ancestors would be to invite misfortune. Some would go much further, and a reluctance to discuss what is known to conflict with Church teaching may only mean that the old concepts and customs have been driven underground. At times of crisis, African Christians may very naturally be drawn to those who seem to understand their real hopes and fears. Hence, as Dr Sundkler says, "Driven underground by the whites, magic is revitalized by the Zionist Church;" and again : "The syncretistic sect becomes the bridge over which Africans are brought back to heathenism." [8]

Fr Thorpe writes : "Hitherto the Church has paid attention to heathen custom only where it impinged on its own discipline—for example, marriage, initiation, and witchcraft. It has neglected the opportunities that are offered by an understanding approach to ancestor-worship and sacrificial customs." An accommodation of Christianity to people of different traditions can never be made at the cost of the dilution of doctrine. Nor can the Church's catholicity give way to tribal or ethnic separatism. But this does not mean that there is no common ground for discussion, or that Christian norms are necessarily Western, still less Anglo-Saxon. What is called for is a living encounter and dialogue between Christian theology and African psychology.

If study of this problem is to be deep enough to be useful it will involve African and white, priest and layman, anthropologist and theologian. Because traditions differ so widely it is a study that will probably have to be done in different areas by different teams of specialists. But it should not be confined to the specialists. Somehow the old atmosphere of denunciation and discipline on the one side and of shame and secrecy on the other must be dissipated, so that people can talk freely about their problems and come to understand them more fully.

The moral for the pastoral work of the Church is that decisions have to be taken out of a living Christian experience, and that they must be decisions, not impositions. John Taylor, writing about Christians of the Rhodesian Copperbelt, considers it questionable whether the modern missionary should ever insist on anything in his own spiritual inheritance which does not compel the conscience of the Church he goes to serve. "For when people do not develop step by step from their point of departure by a series of choices but jump over into an apparently Christian new pattern without growth by decision, then, sooner or later, old pagan patterns reassert themselves."[9]

From the side of Christian theology the attempt to find common ground might begin with a doctrine which links up with the idea of the family extended in time as well as space—the Communion of Saints. A missionary writes: "The relevance of the Feast of the Purification, and, more so, the liturgy for Passion Sunday, to the conversion of Africa can hardly be exaggerated. The significance of the observance of All Saints' and All Souls' when thinking of ancestor-cults is so obvious that one is astounded at the little value that has been placed upon it." Open discussion is better than nominal acceptance of the Christian "No", together with a practical continuance in the old ways. And what of the Christian "Yes"—the sense in which Christ comes not to destroy but to fulfil the deep needs of all mankind? The Christian approach should be humble and sympathetic. The Western world's own past heritage of witchcraft, fear, and superstition may be an asset in this encounter. Christians of every race can say to the Animist, "Our people, too, had ideas like that." And they can preach a Christ who is the liberator from fear.[10]

There are many other problems that call for study and discussion : the recurrent and underlying problem of Western individualism as opposed to African communalism; the differences between Western and African ideas of the numinous; the importance to Africans of dreams and their interpretation; the emphasis placed by Zionists on Moses and John the Baptist and its possible use as a point of contact, and so on. These problems are not theologically irrelevant or pastorally unimportant, nor is there any lack of biblical material bearing upon their study. A missionary writes provocatively about another of these issues, the indigenization of liturgy : "This is obviously so necessary— and yet so full of potential dangers unless it can be worked out by a really well-equipped team of theologians, liturgi-ologists, and African experts—and then, inevitably, the fruits of such a piece of research would be thrown out by the Africans themselves as 'Bantu-ization'; and probably rightly, because liturgical forms must come from below, from the instinctive activity of the worshipping Church. But the longer we allow Anglican chants and a Western structure of liturgy to dominate the scene, the further and further are we taking the worshipping community away from its own culture and situation."

In all this discussion, one principle emerges very clearly : if Christian witness to the heathen is to be effective, great demands will be made on the African congregations, for it is the whole company of the baptized, and not merely the ordained ministers, who are called to be the agents of mission. The instruction of catechumens is therefore very important for the future evangelistic outreach of the Church. Quality matters more than quantity. Yet missionaries are worried already because there is a very large leakage of people who have been attracted to the Faith but who have never got as far as baptism. In the careful selection of candidates for confirmation from those who have "attended classes, put their marriages right, and shown diligence as Christians", the image is projected of a Church strict and respectable, and therefore somewhat off-putting.

How can the Church be widely sympathetic and welcoming, and at the same time vigorously evangelistic through a well-instructed and deeply dedicated laity? This is the sort of question that missionaries are asking, and few would claim that there is an easy answer. Those who pose the question certainly do not ask for any dilution of doctrine, nor for any disparagement of the achievements of the past. "But the case for a reappraisal of our missionary methods and the training of clergy in missionary techniques that will make some impact on the present-day heathen seems to be, to say the least, extremely urgent." Urgent? Yes, indeed. There are three and a half million reasons to prove it.

NOTES

1. Geoffrey Parrinder, *African Traditional Religion*, p. 26.
2. These figures can only be rough estimates. It is estimated that there were 237 million people in Africa in 1959, the annual rate of increase being 1.9 per cent (*United Nations' Demographic Year Book,* 1960). W. T. Harris and E. G. Parrinder suggest that "out of the 137 million or so of Africans South of the Sahara probably at least half are still 'Animists'." Whatever the exact figures, the main point is clear: "for the present, and doubtless for the rest of this century at least, we have to reckon with millions of Animists in Africa." (*The Christian Approach to the Animist*, p. 11.)
3. Leo Marquard, *The Peoples and Policies of South Africa*, p. 233.
4. Philip Mayer, *Townsmen or Tribesmen*, p. 4.
5. Ibid., p. 20.
6. Harris and Parrinder, op. cit., p. 57-62. (The subject of supplementary priests is touched on again in Chapter 10, where reference is made to their use in some other parts of the Anglican Communion.)
7. Geoffrey Parrinder, *African Traditional Religion*, p. 143-4.
8. Bengt Sundkler, *Bantu Prophets in South Africa*. p. 263, 297.
9. J. V. Taylor and Dorothea Lehmann, *Christians of the Copperbelt*, p. 303.
10. Harris and Parrinder, op. cit., p. 59-60.

6

Practical needs to-day

How can we do more effectively what God wants us to do? We may have a vision of a Church alert and active, a Church that God can use; but we want to see some practical steps that we can take in that direction. Here are six needs. If we do our part in meeting them, we shall have moved some distance on the right road, and the way ahead will become clearer.

1. *Prayer* The result of the Church's mission depends on God, not on our cleverness, adaptability, hard work, or sacrificial giving. God calls us to give ourselves in his service, but it is a call to work with him, or rather, to allow him to work through us. Prayer is therefore the indispensable instrument of mission, for it keeps us in living touch with God. It is the Holy Spirit who bears witness to Christ. The Holy Spirit, dwelling in the Church and constituting her life, is a Spirit of witness. Only in the power of the same Holy Spirit can we be Christ's witnesses.

Without prayer we become heavy-footed do-gooders, and probably spend a lot of our time getting in God's way. What we are really seeking is that God's love shall break through. And this will be God's gift when we are ready for it. We shall only be ready if we pray.

"Is he as bad as that?" asked the sick man's wife, when

58

the Rector suggested a prayer. But prayer should be the first resort, not the last. Let us put it first.

2. *Manpower* In *The Moving Spirit*, a survey of the work of the Churches of the Anglican Communion published in 1958, our need for manpower in the Church of the Province is clearly stated : "The shortage of clergy is so serious that many of the bishops refer to it as the main single cause of the failure of the Church to reach out to the unconverted masses" [1] The Report of the Tomlinson Commission, which includes a survey of the work of seventy-eight recognized Churches and missionary societies in what is now the Republic of South Africa, makes the obvious comment, "the results of missions are directly related to the number of missionary workers".[2]

When we take the ministry of the laity seriously it makes a great difference to the work of the ordained clergy; but there remains a need for clergy, and the demand made upon them is all the more searching when the lay-members of the Church are alive to their responsibilities. This points to the need for adequate training, as well as for adequate numbers of men for the ordained ministry.

So, too, with the staffing of mission stations : doctors, matrons, sister-tutors, and nurses; agriculturalists and administrative staff—all these are needed, and it is significant that the supply of such workers comes very largely from the Church in Britain. The Tomlinson Commission found that 68.6 per cent of all the missionaries working in South Africa came from overseas.[3] For our part, we value this partnership very highly; yet it would be wrong for the Church of the Province to expect its missionary work to be done for it. We should rightly expect an increasing number of South Africans to be taking their place, alongside others, in what is after all our own particular field of responsibility. There is a great difference between an appeal from an armchair to the Church in Britain and America, and the call to fellow-workers in another ship to come over and help us with a job that is engaging all our resources to the full.

What would happen if mission hospitals were taken over by the state? Volunteers from overseas would probably prefer to work elsewhere, and if this source of supply dried up there would be a dearth of Christian doctors and nurses working among Africans. Yet the need for Christian workers would be as great as ever.

Mission stations are commonly understaffed. Priests and doctors have to undertake many administrative duties which could be lifted from their shoulders if South Africa was producing its own helpers in sufficient numbers. A priest who has to visit twenty or thirty outstations ought to be able to leave the administrative work in competent hands. Here and there a retired man or woman has proved an enormous asset. On one mission station the electricity plant and the motor transport are in the capable hands of a retired man who finds far more enjoyment in the care of his machines than he would ever get from bowls or bridge.

There is no doubt that sheer ignorance and lack of contact are the causes of our neglect. "We did not know"; again and again this is the summing-up of those who suddenly become aware of the need through a personal visit. Their new-found enthusiasm triggers off an explosion of love and caring—until the chain-reaction gets muffled by the devout and energetic chaos of parish life.

Schoolboys helping Canon Peter Harker in his church-building schemes at Isandlhwana have felt the pull to a life-vocation in the ministry and the mission-field. A visit to Transkei mission stations organized by the Cape Town

Diocesan Board of Missions had the same effect. A young teacher came back from a visit to a mission hospital determined to send hundreds of children's jerseys—because for the first time she had seen the victims of tuberculosis and malnutrition exposed, of necessity, to the cold, fresh, misty air of the Transkei.

It is contact that stirs our imaginations, and our consciences. We need more personal contact, more news, more down-to-earth and detailed information. The reservoir of manpower is there in our membership. When prayerlessness and ignorance are broken down there can be movement instead of stagnation. From praying for missionary needs we go on to learning more about them, and so to working and giving that they may be met. And it is those who pray, work, learn, and give who are ready to hear God's call to go.

3. *Money* Manpower and money go together. When mission stations are inadequately staffed it is largely because the diocese is too poor to provide the people it knows are needed. The range and quality of missionary work are not unrelated to such mundane matters as rands and cents. When a missionary in Basutoland needs a new horse, he can't say to the dealer : "Give me a horse—you'll get your reward in heaven." The dealer wants at least part of it now. What is so important about a horse? There are places up in the mountains where a horse is the only means to carry the ministry of Word and Sacrament—it is, quite simply, an essential instrument of mission.

Part of this financial problem is the disparity in the salaries of the clergy from diocese to diocese. One immediate reaction, no doubt naïve, is to wish that there could be equalization of stipends throughout the Province, irrespective of race. What is certain is that until we grasp this nettle it will go on stinging us. And its sting is too painful to be neglected.

It is possible for a priest in one diocese to receive more by way of the Easter Offering than a priest in another diocese receives as his stipend for the whole year—and, in addition, the first priest's stipend may be very much larger than that of his brother. This seems a particularly unpleasant and unchristian application of the principle that "to him that hath shall be given".

It may happen, too, that a married priest with children to educate works in a diocese where there is no Church school to which he can send them, and yet the Church school in a neighbouring (and richer) diocese is unable to grant him the financial concession given to clergy of that diocese itself who send their children there. It is sometimes said that missionaries can live cheaply; but what about the cost of sending children away as boarders, and the cost of maintaining cars on very punishing roads, and the high cost of petrol and repairs? Modern missionaries do not live an idyllic life of pastoral bliss. They travel a great deal, and they should be able to do so without wondering where the next gallon of petrol is going to come from.

A married priest who has mastered an African language and is becoming really useful as a missionary may have to leave simply because he cannot afford to educate his children. This is, quite simply, wasteful. Nobody should speak lightly of "the children having to make sacrifices" who has not faced such a situation himself.

Of course, this problem is far from simple. The question of diocesan autonomy is involved in it. We may say that a diocese should not become autonomous until it is financially viable, but the fact is that there is a very great

disparity of resources between *existing* dioceses.[4] Surely
fellowship should be a stronger reality than diocesan autonomy? Surely we ought to be able to deal with this problem
on a Provincial basis, so that we may bring to an end the
present situation, by which the ministry is denied to places
where it is most needed.

Equally difficult is the question of the differential between the salaries of white and African clergy. Some
dioceses with a few African clergy have found it possible to
reduce the differential or even to eliminate it. Others,
where African clergy are in the majority, would have to
cut their staff drastically, or else find large new financial
resources. The differential is sometimes defended on the
ground that it avoids the danger of African clergy becoming comparatively rich men in their own community. This
argument might have more force if it were the custom for
a white priest in a slum parish to come under comparable
financial restrictions. Such a priest, of course, makes very
considerable sacrifices, but his *stipend* is the same as that of
another white priest in a wealthy parish in the same
diocese.

Again, it is very doubtful whether clergy, on the best
stipends at present available in the Province, would in fact
be wealthy compared with African lawyers, doctors, school-
principals, and business men. Yet any change in this
differential would inevitably raise the problem of the very
small remuneration given to African preachers and catechists, who form the front line in the out-stations. And
would the parishes be willing to accept higher assessments,
and would they be able to meet them?

There is, to-day, a fairly widespread and growing conviction about the need for parity of clerical stipends, but

there are still great differences of opinion about the speed with which parity is to be achieved.

What is quite clear is that it would be very unfair to expect the poorer dioceses to deal with this matter on their own. There is the plainest possible need for partnership and fellowship throughout the Province as we tackle one of the most difficult of all our problems.

Financial needs are a limiting factor, too, in the training of clergy and catechists, and only the best use of our available resources will meet the case. Where is the money to come from? As with manpower, so with money: it is only when we have learned to give sacrificially ourselves that we have the right to call upon the gifts of others.

4. *Vocation and training* The idea of vocation must not be limited to a few "professional" jobs in the service of the Church. To have a vocation—to be called by God— is to know his will to bring us into living relationship with himself and into the community of his people. We are "called to be saints" (Rom. 1.7)—to be redeemed and sanctified members of the Body of Christ. This is *the* vocation of Christians, and it is common to them all.

It is only on this basis that the further calling of Christians can be understood—the calling to live in responsible obedience to God wherever we may be in the world, and to be ready to obey his summons to any particular task whenever it may come.[5]

But the special calling *does* come to many of us, and because we are aware of the challenge of Christian vocation in the widest context of the world's life we cannot neglect the call to the ordained ministry or to service as a missionary doctor, nurse, administrator, or agriculturist.

We have seen that the Province may very rightly be

expected to produce an increasing proportion of its workers, while fully aware of its fellowship in a world-wide Communion. We have noticed, too, the need for contact, understanding, and first-hand experience if vocations are to be fostered. But side by side with vocation goes training. The point is made in *Missionary Commitments of the Anglican Communion* that "the essentials for a status of genuine self-support are present when the episcopate and the clergy and the means for training the clergy are found from resources within the country itself. This is not to say that most valuable aid cannot be given from one Church to another through men and women whose support is provided by the 'sending' not the 'receiving' Church. What is vital, however, in these days of nationalist revolt against outside domination is that each Church should be in secure possession of the resources for maintaining the essentials of its life." [6]

In the past, many ordinands have been sent overseas for training. This may have the unfortunate effect of giving the impression to those who are trained in South Africa that they have somehow failed to make the grade, and may retard the full development of our own theological colleges. It would seem logical that most of our ordinands should be trained in their home country, and that overseas visits should be used chiefly for specialized courses after a few years of experience—for example, at St Augustine's, Canterbury. Certainly we should do all in our power to raise and train the ministry we need, and it is encouraging to know that the syllabus of training and the length of the course are at present under review.

For the training of lay missionaries we have no facilities in South Africa, and this is a glaring weakness. We need, at the very least, a hostel associated with a university which offers courses in theology, African languages, and social anthropology, so that doctors, nurses, and others can prepare for missionary service without the great expense of a training overseas.

5. *Penetration*   It is an Anglo-Saxon attitude not to be too enthusiastic. Is there a possibility that we are not using to the full our existing resources because we are too nice, too restrained to do so? Writing of these immediate needs, a missionary says: "I should have placed first conviction and conversion with reference to the ministry." Our clergy need to be, themselves, convinced and converted Christians, and they need the "instinct of conquest" which is essential if the powers of evil are to be pushed back and the frontiers of God's realm extended.

No doubt a missionary doctor or nurse serves God primarily by efficient and selfless performance of medical duties. But every missionary—indeed, every Christian—should be a "speaking witness" too. It is only missionaries themselves who can say whether or not we are failing in this regard. At least it is clear that the "incarnation" of mission through acts of identification and through institutions does not absolve us from the need to penetrate and to evangelize, so that God may change people from the inside out. "Woe is me if I preach not the Gospel," said St Paul; and every great missionary has had this divine discontent, this single-minded aim.

6. *Province-wide commitment*   In the Anglican Communion as a whole we have begun to see the development of an overall strategic concept. The appointment of Bishop Stephen Bayne as Executive Officer and the attention given to missionary strategy at the Lambeth Conference of 1958 are signs of this desire to think and act together and with

maximum effect. The Church of the Province has followed the same path in providing for a Provincial Executive Officer and a Provincial Board of Missionary Strategy. What the Lambeth Conference said of the whole Communion is also true of the Province : "it needs to be reminded in all its parts that no one lives to himself, and that as a body with a common life the whole is always something greater than the sum of those parts." [7]

Growth often involves death. The adolescent "dies" that the adult may live. There has to be a death to bachelor egoism if marriage is to succeed. Christians learn that there must be a death to self, in order that we may live to Christ and to each other. So, too, the call may come for a death to parochialism, and to the sort of autonomy that denies fellowship.

The problems of manpower and money—so closely related—can only be dealt with as the whole Province faces its needs with the determination that they shall be met. The training of clergy and lay-workers is a Provincial problem. These are not *chiefly* matters of machinery; they call for a new sense of solidarity and a far greater caring one for another than we have been accustomed to show.

But some machinery there must be. It is arguable that we are over-organized. Committees increase in number, and the fact that the same people serve on a great many of them makes them burdensome and tends to interrupt the pastoral ministry. The load should be spread as widely as possible. But when this has been said, we have to recognize, too, that the forwarding of the Church's mission calls for corporate thought, decision, and action. Unless there is in each diocese something in the nature of a Board of Mission, it seems likely that we shall be more inclined to muddle along than to face our problems.

No doubt the functions of such organizations will differ according to the local need. A missionary writes : "Most parishes and mission districts in South Africa are too incoherent for much to be done on a parochial scale. A parish where there are about a dozen of the faithful, as there are in many dorps, can be tackled only from a diocesan centre." Here there is a need for executive action. In other areas the primary task may be missionary education and the calling out of support from those who are only too prone to ignore their responsibilities. And everywhere there will be the need to stimulate evangelism and to set forward the mission of the Church in and through the parishes.

It all comes down to the parish in the end, for there the Christian learns his faith and there he must live it out. It is the parishes alone that can make the Province what it ought to be.

NOTES

1. *The Moving Spirit*, p. 85.
2. *Summary of the Report of the Commission for the Socio-economic Development of the Bantu Areas within the Union of South Africa*, p. 22.
3. Ibid., p. 56.
4. Compare the Anglican Church of Canada, where out of twenty-eight dioceses fourteen are described as "missionary" in the sense that they require help from outside both in manpower and money. Grants made to these fourteen dioceses by the Missionary Society of the Church in Canada totalled 350,000 dollars in 1955 (*Missionary Commitments of the Anglican Communion*, p. 16).

5. See articles, "Call", in *A Theological Word Book of the Bible*, p. 39; "Vocation", in *A Handbook of Christian Theology*, p. 373.
6. *Missionary Commitments of the Anglican Communion*, p. 12.
7. *The Lambeth Conference*, 1958, p. 2. 69.

7

The Parish: Training for Mission

PARISHES differ in all sorts of ways, but there is one principle that we should expect to find acknowledged in every parish except a dead one—its partnership in the missionary work of the Province. The needs of dioceses like St John's, Zululand and Swaziland, Damaraland, Basutoland, and Lebombo are so obvious that we feel ashamed if we are doing nothing to help. Every other diocese of the Province, too, has work that we immediately recognize as a direct fulfilment of the Church's mission. Such work makes a claim upon our prayers and gifts, and the basis of this claim is not romanticism—it is the sheer fact that we are in this thing together.

It would be ridiculous to argue that because the mission of the Church is inseparable from its being in every place there are therefore no places of special opportunity and need. That would be like saying that because charity begins at home it must stay there too. Mission beyond one's own immediate surroundings remains a distinctive element in the total Christian mission: not the whole of it certainly, not even a superior part of it; but nevertheless essential to a vigorous Christian life.

The realization of this partnership by Christians who are themselves struggling to present the Gospel to great numbers of pagan Africans puts to shame the complacency of many a parish in the cities and the suburbs. The Bishop of Zululand and Swaziland writes: "It is now official diocesan policy to try to give our Lent Offerings outside the diocese. We feel that we must be givers as well as receivers, however poor we may be." In 1961 a total of R924 was sent to the Boys' Hostel at Kurnool in the Nandyal area of South India. The following year the offerings went to the diocese of Nyasaland, whose bishop, the Right Reverend Donald Arden, had recently served as a missionary in Swaziland.

Yet this principle of care for other Christians—taught by St Paul, practised in the early Church, accepted to-day wherever the Christian community is conscious of its fellowship in world-wide mission—has been forgotten in many places. It is a fact that one of the greatest differences between parishes is precisely this, that some are keenly and willingly committed to missionary responsibility, while others seem never to think beyond the annual bazaar, the church roof, the organ, or the new vestry. Some parishes give regularly for missionary work. A few give sacrificially. Others give very little, and then it is done as if it were an occasional afterthought. The proportion of giving and even the total amount seem to bear very little relation to the wealth of a particular parish. Prayer for missionary work and interest in learning about it appear to vary just as widely.

It is tempting to think that if we are to see the resources of the whole Church mobilized it will have to be done by legislation—by organizing a unitary missionary agency or some sort of quota system for the Province as a whole. But "the centralizing of missionary organization is no guarantee whatever that the missionary concern will be central in the life of the Church." [1] In fact, there is evidence that to turn missionary support from a duty to a tax merely makes it as impersonal and uninteresting as any other tax, and perhaps as unpopular too.[2] Besides, the Christian mission depends on more than money. It needs sustained prayer, a deep sense of partnership, and a constant flow of recruits. What we need is a new outlook; but how is it to be achieved?

How, in practice, *does* a parish become missionary-minded? What makes it begin to face outwards to the non-Christian world around it, and show an active concern for missionary work throughout the Province and beyond, while a neighbouring parish may face inwards and be preoccupied with its own survival? Somehow a missionary tradition grows up, fires people's imaginations, and begins to shape their activity. It is the old story of the leaven in the lump. It needs one enthusiast to start off with, preferably the Rector. Then around the one enthusiast there gathers a group of people willing to pray, work, learn, and give. They may become the nucleus of a parochial missionary association. But their work is only beginning until they have made the whole parish, from the Sunday School to the Church Council, aware of the demands of mission and glad to accept its responsibilities. The aim is not to create additional organizations, but to make the existing organizations more fruitful and effective. The test comes, perhaps, when the Rector leaves. If the parish is really alive the work will go on.

Does it seem too early to begin in the Sunday School? Perhaps we ought to ask whether it can ever be too early to teach the right idea of the Church. The wrong idea, once learned, may never be unlearned. Confirmation preparation is a second great opportunity. We often complain that Confirmation becomes a formality, an end instead of a beginning, and that the clergy present to the bishop far too many candidates who are already on the way to becoming lapsed communicants. But the fault may lie in the training. Unless it is training for life, for witness, for mission, it may well be training for passivity and death.

Often, too, in a parish there is no group which can be joined by young people who really mean business—the sort of group to which the more challenging demands of vocation and consecration can be put. Young men and women do not want to be soothed with slight demands and limited to small horizons. They will respond to the implicit assumption that each of them is seeking a worth-while aim in life and a particular fulfilment of Christian vocation. We ought not to complain of lack of leaders if we never train any. Our senior Bible Class, Youth Club, or A.Y.P.A. should do more than keep young people off the streets. It should be the place where militant Christians get their training for life.

The truth is that mission doesn't just happen. There must be the enthusiast to put it across, the "ginger group" to jog the whole parish out of its complacency, and then a continuing process of education for mission, so that the vision does not fade. Sermons, meetings, films, talks, literature, drama—there are many means we can use. The possibility of visits to mission stations should not be overlooked. The casual "rubberneck" who calls in and wants to be shown around must be an infuriating distraction to the busy missionary. But a pre-arranged visit, organized to minimize the burden of hospitality and to stimulate the direct support of the mission by those who take part and those whom they can influence when they get back home, will almost invariably be welcomed.

Yet even this realization of partnership is only the first stage of training for mission. In the infinite variety of parish life all things are possible. It is possible (however perverse it may seem) for a parish to develop great enthusiasm for the support of missionary work in distant places, and *at the same time to ignore and neglect the challenge on its own doorstep*. Distance lends enchantment. The romance of faraway places with unpronounceable names can be a substitute for the hard realism of our duty to the everyday world that lies so near at hand. We have to come back again and again to the realization that the Church has one mission, and that it must fulfil this mission in every place.

We can no longer be content to behave as though missionary work in Vendaland or Ovamboland had nothing to do with the preaching of the Gospel and the life of the Christian community in the city or the suburb or the country district where we live. Education for mission must therefore seek to break down the middle walls of partition. We do not need a unified quota system to extract our money while leaving us no better informed and no more closely involved than we were before; but we may well need a unified *missionary education* which is realistic and not romantic, which recalls Christians to their own mission at the same time as it reveals the nature of the Church's mission in other places.

The Protestant Episcopal Church of America has recently decided to take action along these lines. Every year a theme is chosen, around which a parish programme can be designed. Provision is made for different age-groups in the parish, so that each can gain a fresh understanding of Christian mission and relate it to local needs and the needs of the Church at large.

First of all each Rector is asked to select a group of people to work with him for a period of six to eight weeks to plan for the parish. A training guide is provided. Then a Missionary Education Portfolio for the year is issued—a packet containing study material for all ages. For adults, there is a series of studies on "You, your Church, and your Job," bringing out the relation between worship and daily life in the world.

There is also study material on a selected mission-field, for example, Latin America. Children and young people follow the same theme, but with a special approach suitable for each group.

It is clear that in any parish where this method is used there will be a growing understanding of the mission of the laity from Monday to Saturday, a growing realization that other people in other places and under different conditions participate in the same mission, and the discovery that there are ways in which each can be of service to the other as *together* they obey the Great Commission of Christ. This is an idea we could well copy from our fellow-Anglicans of the American Church, adapting it to the needs of a Province with great mission-fields inside its own borders.[3]

There is, of course, no need to wait for the provision of such an organized scheme, however much we should appreciate it. As Douglas Webster writes: "Every local congregation has to be made profoundly and disturbingly aware of what is happening in the whole world and in the whole Church. That is what missionary education is all about. It may be helpful to regard it as quadrilateral, the four points of its programme being a truer understanding of the world, the Church, the Bible and the liturgy. For the world is the context of mission, the Church is the instrument of mission, the Bible is the basis of mission, and the liturgy should be the inspiration of mission. Each of these items is an area of Christian study in its own right. Missionary education is the compound of all four, the constant bringing of them together and showing their relationships, the bearing of the one upon the rest." [4]

The means of missionary education are near at hand, but they are largely unused. This is particularly true of the Bible. Douglas Webster writes again : "The Bible is absolutely basic to missionary education. It is the study of the Bible that has been responsible for every great missionary movement in the history of the Church. . . . Whilst it is true to say that no Church in Christendom gives a greater place to the reading of the Bible in its public services of worship than our Anglican Church, it may also be true to say that no Church has so large a proportion of its members so abysmally ignorant of the Bible's teaching. And if the tendency to shorter and shorter sermons is allowed to go unchecked and the only ministry of the Word our people receive is a three minute chat tagged on to seven minutes of largely futile notices at the Parish Communion, then there is not the slightest hope of our Churchpeople becoming literate Christians or of our Church itself being able to carry out, let alone extend, its enormous missionary commitments." [5]

He adds that his own conviction is that every parish should have something in the nature of a Bible school, meeting once a week through the major part of the year, and that the parish priest should give time for this whatever else he has to cut out.

For many people this idea of a Bible school sounds hopelessly old-fashioned and quite out of touch with the businesslike methods of the mid-twentieth century. But in fact it is this opinion which is old-fashioned. It might have

been more persuasive when theology was in its liberal hey-
day and the Church was hesitant and apologetic about the
Bible. Reeling from the impact of evolutionary theory and
the radical methods of critical scholarship, Christians
were understandably on the defensive when they opened
the old Book. The Modernist movement tried to meet the
intellectual challenge on its own ground. The fundamentalist reaction drew the lines of battle in a different place,
defending the authority of the Word of God by a vigorous
repudiation of the tendency to treat it just like any other
literature. But in the struggle both camps lost the sense
that the Bible has a message for the contemporary world
and its problems.[6]

Bible study *was* dull and out of date when the Bible was
treated either as a compendium of primitive religion or as
a repository of proof-texts. Then came the great assertion
of Karl Barth that "the Bible could not be read like any
other historical material. . . . The Bible should be read as
an urgent message addressed to individual men and women
—'to me with my name on it'." [7] And the Bible became a
living book once more to people who had found no inspiration in the controversy of liberal versus fundamentalist.
Members of the Confessing Church in Germany under the
Nazis found that the Bible spoke directly to their condition.
A new interest in Bible study was brought to the student
world through gifted interpreters, among whom the names
of Visser 't Hooft and Suzanne de Diétrich stand out.
Christians learned to see the Bible whole, and the drama
of God's redemptive activity in history became enthrall-
ingly real and relevant.

It is because biblical theology has still not reached down
to parish level in many places that Bible study can seem
stuffy and unattractive even to-day. The great message of

God's concern for his world remains unread in a Book that reposes among the family heirlooms in many homes and is never opened except to record a birth, a marriage, or a death. "I like to keep a Bible in the house," said one woman, "it brings good luck." It is the clergy who must open the Bible to the people by their preaching and teaching, so that the Bible in the parish and the Bible in the home can become the focus for Christian thinking and Christian action.

People to-day pride themselves on being practical, and it is arguable that some of the energy which should have been devoted to this new and exciting study of the Bible has been channelled into planned giving campaigns, which ring more bells in the mind of the Organization Man. These campaigns have done a great deal of good, even apart from their financial results. Membership becomes real instead of merely nominal when the needs of the Church are taken seriously and a corporate effort is made to meet them.

Christian stewardship can be a means of mission when it shows that membership of Christ in his Church is not a superficial fellowship, but a common life of mutual responsibility. The very fact that the inner nucleus moves out to the people on the fringe is a denial of the ghetto mentality.

A layman knocking on doors in a parish in the Cape Peninsula was greeted with the words, "Ah, you're just the chap I've been wanting to see. What's all this about the Father, the Son, and the Holy Ghost?" Doctrine comes alive when you have to explain it yourself. And the uselessness of much of our ecclesiastical jargon and the irrelevance of many of our parochial habits can no longer be concealed when the people from the centre and the people on the fringe get together.

But Christian stewardship, too, can be side-tracked into a cul-de-sac. There are three dangers. First, the planned giving system may become a *substitute,* not only for Bible study, but for mission itself. Canvassing and re-canvassing involves a lot of hard work, enough to fill the limited spare time of the keen nucleus. Yet this can never be the whole work of the Church, nor can it absolve us from the necessity to penetrate, evangelize, and transform the world. Secondly, the stress on money may become too *exclusive.* A rich Church can lose its way. To such a Church it was said once, "While you say, 'I am rich, I have prospered, and there is nothing that I need,' you have no eyes to see that you are wretched, pitiable, poverty-stricken, blind, and naked. My advice to you is to buy from me that gold which is purified in the furnace so that you may be rich, and white garments to wear so that you may hide the shame of your nakedness, and salve to put on your eyes to make you see." (Rev. 3. 17-18.) Thirdly, unless there is a real sense of partnership the greater resources of the well-organized parishes will bring no comfort to those who have to do pioneering work in lonely places with no great reservoir of material support from which to draw.

At the New Delhi Assembly of the World Council of Churches, Dr Paul Devanandan spoke on the theme, *Called to Witness.* He said, "But consider how much of our energy is consumed in 'drives' and 'campaigns' *to consolidate the traditional patterns of congregational life".*[8] This is the danger : we may use new techniques to pursue outdated objectives. To measure success in terms of numbers, prosperity, and prestige is to be conformed to the pattern of this world. Christ's way is the way of service and of suffering. It is the way of the grain of wheat that dies in order that it may bear much fruit.

There are many parishes, with an apparently flourishing programme, which show very little evidence of Christian community and Christian responsibility. Their people come and go like the members of a successful club, and their activities are a sort of bowdlerized version of club activities decorated with a veneer of respectability. In one Church— a flourishing and active one—an adult discussion-group spent an evening considering the agonizing problems of Christian disunity. Three speakers of different traditions had their say. Tea was served. Then questions were invited. After a long pause, a member of the audience got up. "I have a question," he said, "Would anyone like another cup of tea?"

The modern cult of the soothing cup of tea is a far cry from the fellowship meal of the early church. A layman in a London parish once suggested that the Church should adopt its own flag: green to represent the earth, blue to represent heaven, and against this background a cup of tea rampant, as the main means of getting from the one to the other. We must be careful that the challenge of Christian reponsibility is not lost among the teacups or swilled down the sink.

Planned giving can easily become the means to even greater comfort for the already comfortable: yet it clearly implies, and should involve, a partnership with those who work on the frontiers, far from the encouragements of the well-supplied base. In every campaign this fact should be recognized, and a generous proportion of the money pledged and given to the Church should be sent where it is needed most.

Unless this missionary partnership is understood from the beginning, it becomes very difficult to find room for it later on. A pattern has been established. The parish is working for itself, and when the vestry has been enlarged there is always another object in view—to move the organ, perhaps, or to modernize the Church Hall. By an extension of Parkinson's Law projects proliferate to use up the available income. In themselves they may be worthy, and even necessary, but they should never be met by cutting off the supply to the Church's outposts—a supply that can come only from the established parishes. This principle is all the more important because planned giving promises to eliminate extra appeals; and to offer a missionary box to someone who has already pledged a comprehensive amount is both tactless and unfair.

When these dangers are avoided, Christian stewardship campaigns have immense possibilities for good. They encourage the outward look, the active fellowship, and the realization of the full potential of a parish. They involve training, discussion, lay-activity, movement, contact. It is a fact that the missionary societies in Britain are gaining a great measure of new support from parishes which practice planned giving in some form. The same benefit could come to the predominantly missionary dioceses of the Church of the Province from parishes all over South Africa. The need is very great, and very urgent.

There is, of course, no contradiction between this sense of missionary partnership and an attitude of alertness to local needs. When a parish really comes alive it finds itself actively involved in mission to its own immediate neighbourhood no less than in mission throughout the Province. There is no Church, however prosperous or long-established, that is not living in a missionary situation. Its own local environment is its primary mission-field. The help it gives to those further away leaves the initiative with them. But here, in the parish itself, it is the Christian community centred in the parish church that must accept the responsibility and exercise the initiative. This is why there must be training for mission—and why the training must be put into practice.

NOTES

1. Douglas Webster, *Missionary Societies—One or Many?*, p. 9.
2. Douglas Webster makes the point that the Protestant Episcopal Church of America has had a quota system for missionary giving since 1919, yet the need has now been felt for a voluntary Overseas Mission Society "devoted to recalling the Church to the centrality of its Mission".
3. Articles in *Christian Education Findings*, May, 1961; September, 1961; December, 1961.
4. Douglas Webster, *Local Church and World Mission*, p. 10.
5. Ibid., p. 55.
6. E. H. Robertson, *The Bible in Our Time: The Recovery of Confidence*, p. 14.
7. Ibid., p. 16-17.
8. Assembly Document 3, p. 4 (italics added).

8

The Ministry of the Laity

WHEN we accept the fact that we are involved in mission *here,* where we live and work, the question at once arises : where are the local missionaries, the Christian militants? The simple answer is, they are in the pews. The laity, it has been said, are the frozen assets of the Church. To-day there are signs of a thaw. There may be a few burst pipes here and there, but there are also the beginnings of activity and movement.

The blessing at the end of the service was never meant to be a sort of signing-off until we meet again next week, same time, same place. It is more like the marching-orders of Christ's army, as we go out into Christ's world to work and to witness for him. Throughout the world to-day Christians are accepting this vision of the Church Militant as a welcome change from a conventional, passive Churchianity. It is a change that could be revolutionary, for it implies the end of all those varieties of formalism which so effectively anaesthetize the devout laity and repel the outsider.

So far, it is true, the appeal to the laity for their commitment to the mission of the Church has been chiefly opportunistic or pragmatic. As Hendrik Kraemer points out, it has happened as a result of the increasing recognition, by many Churches, of their evangelistic and missionary responsibility to their environment. The clergy know that they cannot meet these needs alone. They call on the laity for help. But such help is very often envisaged, by priest and layman alike, as a lifting of the particular burdens of the priesthood. Laymen are regarded as having fulfilled their function when they have become auxiliary Church workers. We are inclined to regard the "good Churchman" as someone who is already a little like a priest. This does not take us very far from the old idea that women can follow their Christian calling by "doing the flowers", organizing cake-sales, and making up a quorum for week-day services.

Kraemer maintains that it is our secularized mode of thinking that makes us easily a prey to the habit of seeing affairs of religion and the Church as a matter for clergy and theologians, whereas the rôle of the laity naturally finds its explanation in the political and social spheres.[1] Such a divided view of life is quite un-Christian. What is really called for, he suggests, is a new ecclesiology—a new doctrine of the Church. As Fr Congar has put it, "Fundamentally there is but one valid theology of the laity; that is to say, a whole ecclesiology." [2]

This need becomes apparent when we realize how the word "laity" has been debased from its original meaning of "the chosen people of God" to mean "those who are non-clerical" or "those who are non-professional". In some contexts "layman" now means one unqualified to speak or judge. It is perhaps a sign of the common acceptance of this debasement that a synod of clergy is often called a Sacred Synod. How can it be any more sacred than a synod with lay-representatives?

We need to get away from the tendency to define the laity negatively, as those who are not clergy. Certainly, "to be a layman means to be part of God's Mission to the world." [3] But more than this : the Church's mission is carried out *primarily* by the laity, and the main area of that mission is the world where men and women live and work. The laity is that part of the Church which has to carry the brunt of the encounter with the world in and around themselves, and to voice and incarnate Christ's relevance to the whole range of human life.

It is true, of course, that when laymen become more active as voluntary Church workers—as visitors, street wardens, hosts of the House Church, and so on—the priest is free to be the priest. This is a great gain. But it is not because it helps the clergy that the work of the laity needs to be properly understood : it is because it fulfils the mission of the Church. The New Testament standard is a high one : "You are a chosen race, a royal priesthood, a holy nation, God's own people, that you may declare the wonderful deeds of him who called you out of darkness into his marvellous light." (1 Peter 2, 9.)

What we need, then, is a new vision of the Church, in which the laity gets its full meaning. For if the life of the Church is to involve training for active participation in mission by all its members, it will make a difference to everything. There may have to be changes in the parish pattern—a greater realism, more scope for lay initiative, a decrease in harmless but irrelevant club activity. (Perhaps it is not always harmless. As Thoreau pointed out, you can't kill time without injuring eternity.)

In the word "laity" men and women are equally included. The "man" in "layman" has a generic and not a sexual significance. Yet the Church has been slow and reluctant to recognize the fact that in this sense, as in others, man embraces woman. The exclusion of women from synods is surely based on an anomalous and indefensible

85

conservatism. Professional women workers in the Church should have the status, salary, and security which will enable them to follow their vocation without avoidable frustration and anxiety. Clergy pensions may not be very wonderful, but women workers often have none at all. And we should give up trying to turn every Lydia into a Dorcas. There are Christian women whose particular gifts are not being used, simply because they are women.

These changes of attitude are a matter of immediate and urgent concern, for this is a problem that shows itself in all our Church life. In settled parishes and missionary outposts alike we suffer from the passivity of the laity. It is not that they do not support the clergy. It is, rather, that they seem too dependent on the clergy. Perhaps the clergy like to have it that way. An old priest of great experience was heard to mutter one day, "The trouble is the clergy don't really believe that the laity have the Holy Spirit." Of course, the laity should be able to rely on the clergy to fulfil their particular function in the Church. But they should not be taught to rely on the clergy for everything. Their true source of strength is the working of the Holy Spirit in themselves.

This is the burden of Roland Allen's book, *Missionary Methods: St Paul's or Ours?"* It is a book that has to be read with caution. It is a sustained piece of special pleading. It idealizes the early Church. It ignores the fact that St Paul was able to utilize the Jewish Dispersion and the Synagogue almost everywhere he went.[5] On its appearance fifty years ago it aroused a great deal of resentment. Yet its message is more readily understood to-day, though it is no easier to accept.

Roland Allen was dissatisfied with the strategic concept of contemporary missions. Missionaries in his day liked to occupy important centres, and there to establish settled institutions. But "there is no particular virtue in attacking a centre or establishing a Church in an important place unless the Church established in the important place is a Church possessed of sufficient life to be a source of light to the whole country round." [6] St Paul also had "strategic centres", but they were strategic because he made them so : "They were not centres at which he must stop, but centres from which he might begin; not centres into which life drained, but centres from which it spread abroad." [7] "Concentrated missions at strategic centres, if they are to win the province, must be centres of evangelistic life." [8]

St Paul did not scatter the seed of the Gospel vaguely and generally : he brought people to the point of decision, a decision through which a man came into contact with the divine source of life. In vital union with Christ, the Christian knew himself to be a member of a fully organized indigenous Church, in which he shared the evangelistic task committed by Christ to his apostles. "St Paul was always calling out more and more the capacities of the people in the Church." [9] "His converts became missionaries. . . . This surprises us : we are not always accustomed to find our converts so zealous. Yet it is not really surprising. Christians receive the Spirit of Jesus, and the Spirit of Jesus is the missionary spirit, the Spirit of him who came into the world to bring back lost souls to the Father. Naturally when they receive that Spirit they begin to seek to bring others back, even as he did." [10]

St Paul established firmly the great principle of mutual responsibility in the life of the Church. Roland Allen thought that somehow this had been lost. "Dependence does not train for independence," he warned, and again and again he asserted : "Christians are not only what they are by nature, they are a Spirit-bearing body. It is not a question merely of our faith in them: it is still more a question of faith in the Holy Ghost." [11]

The report, *Towards the Conversion of England*, prefaced a chapter on "The apostolate of the whole Church" with a quotation from William Temple: "The evangelization of England . . . is a work that cannot be done by the clergy alone; it can only be done to a very small extent by the clergy at all. There can be no widespread evangelization of England unless the work is undertaken by the lay people of the Church. . . . The main duty of the clergy must be to train the lay members of the congregation in their work of witness." [12] The fact that this view is now being taken seriously is evident again and again in modern literature on the Church's mission. In the symposium *Part-Time Priests?*, for example, the Bishop of Bath and Wells writes: "Very little consideration has been given to the place and function of the laity in the life of the Church except under commissioned services. And yet every lay person in the congregation is a potential evangelist, if he is prepared to be trained and to apply himself to that task." [13] It is pointed out that the effectiveness of sects like Jehovah's Witnesses is largely due to the fact that they expect all their members to be active agents.

The Bishop of Michigan writes: "Before we can grow and grasp our opportunity we must rid our minds of the one-man army assumption, and we must see with penitence that we tend to be a clerically dominated Church."[14] It is not that the clergy are tyrants, but simply that they are trying to do too much themselves. Yet, as George Goyder says, "When the clergy bring themselves to trust the laity, the laity will begin to trust themselves to be the Church." [15]

Again, Bishop Barry writes of the need to learn "to deploy our total ministry"—to use fully the sum of ministerial resources which are inherent in the Church itself. "What we need," he writes, "is to rediscover the laity as the people of God who *are* the Church and are, therefore, called as Christians to take part in its ministry and priestly function." [16]

It is significant that the mobilization of the laity becomes a recurrent theme in a book which is primarily a discussion of new patterns for the life of the ordained ministry. The ministry of the clergy and the ministry of the laity are seen to be inseparably connected in the total mission of the Church. We cannot reassess the rôle of one without also studying the rôle of the other. "The function and activity of the ordained clergy as integrated with that of the laity is the basic question": in these words a South African missionary of wide experience puts his finger on the spot. It has been said that to-day the priest must learn to be chaplain to the priestly laity. This is true, but the truth is more complex than this. For there is an element of authority inseparable from the ordained ministry. The problem is how to exercise this authority in terms not of lordship but of humble service—how to delegate and share responsibility within the one body of the Church: and how to do this without allowing the fellowship of the Church to be equated with the democratic ideals of secularized society.

The Reverend A. G. Hebert dealt with this point in a paper read as long ago as 1941. Writing of the community and fellowship which is proper to the Church, he claimed that it is as different from democracy, in its ordinary secular meaning, as it is from the ordinary, secular meaning of autocracy. "There is indeed an element in the Christian calling which constitutes the truth that underlies Democracy. It is possible for a cobbler not only to be a good Christian, in the ordinary sense, but also to have a soundness and maturity of spiritual judgement which makes his opinion really weighty in all matters which come within the range of his knowledge. But this does not mean that the Church can be in the ordinary sense 'democratic'. allowing individuals and parties to claim a *right* to put forward individual and personal views and seek to make them prevail by a majority vote. According to her view of things, no one has any *right* to be listened to, except in so far as he has been taught by the Holy Spirit; and then it is the *duty* of everyone in the assembly to attend very seriously to what he has been given to say. For the aim of the assembly is to reach a common mind, based on a real understanding of the principles which the various members have been seeking to assert; and it is this common mind that the individual contributions are intended to build up.

But such an understanding of one another's mind presupposes a common faith—that is, a fundamental agreement about the way of looking at things; and this in turn implies that each local unit of the Church needs to have in it someone armed with apostolic authority and responsible for the exposition of the faith—the bishop in a diocese, the priest in a parish. As then there is in the Church a 'democratic' element, so there is an 'autocratic' element: the bishop and the priest have received a commission which is not of man nor from man, and it is not to man that they are responsible for the exercise of their authority. They must then accept responsibility for their decisions; they can never be subject to a committee in those matters which belong to their ministerial office." [17]

As Fr Hebert saw so clearly, there is always a real danger that the element of authority will become a worldly autocracy, just as the element of fellowship can degenerate into a worldly democratic spirit. There seems to be no escape from corruption *so long as we keep the Church in the centre of our thinking.* For the truth is that the Church was never meant to be the centre. Christ is the centre, and the Church exists for the sake of the world.[18] It looks as if ecclesiology is meant to be discovered *en passant,* as we fulfil our mission.

Dr J. C. Hoekendijk's assertion that interest in the Church is generally a sign of spiritual tiredness deserves careful consideration. "The Church-centric conception," he writes, " . . . has clasped us so tight, has so spun its web about us that we ourselves hardly realize how far the Churchification of our thought has gone. From this crushing embrace we shall never escape, until we learn to ask again and most seriously what it means when we repeat again and again our beloved missionary text, 'This Gospel of the Kingdom must be preached in all the world,' and to attempt to find our solution of the problem of the Church in this framework of Kingdom-Gospel-Witness (apostolate)-world." [19]

When the Church accepts its mission and is active in the fulfilment of its responsibility to the world, the tension between clergy and laity falls away. There is no longer any danger of their competing for authority in a static organization : they are partners in an outgoing enterprise. The teaching function of the ordained minister is no longer practised on an inert or resentful laity : it is the layman who comes back from his encounter with the world *asking* for expert advice.

We need a mission concept of the priesthood as part of the mission concept of the whole Church, a point well brought out in the writings of the Abbé Michonneau. The priest cannot lead his army from behind. In fact, it has been the dominant experience of the Church in France that mission is to be fulfilled not by the individual, whether priest or layman, but by the *team*. Canon Cardijn, the founder of the Jocists, writes : "It is not a question of forming individuals, it is a question of forming teams. Apostles cannot be formed singly." [20] And the Abbé Michonneau states emphatically : "it is the idea of the team which has struck the deepest roots in us and done the most to prove itself." [21]

The leadership of the clergy is needed, as well as the active participation of the laity, if we are to hear what God is saying to his Church to-day. The Holy Spirit is at work, and his aim seems to be to turn the parish inside out. New life is sweeping through the Christian world in the emphasis on biblical theology and liturgical reform, in the development of the House Church, in the Ecumenical Movement, and in and through all this in the deployment of the Church's members for the fulfilment of their mission. Some of the benefits of this new thinking are being brought to the Church of the Province through *Faith in Action,* a non-party movement of clergy and laity which has grown up to foster a fresh understanding of the Christian faith and to put it into practice. It often happens that the winds of new thinking blow right over the institutional Church, which huddles down in cosy complacency. *Faith in Action* encourages us to open the windows and doors and let the fresh air in.

There is a growing conviction to-day that the disturbing breath of the Spirit is urging the Christian laity to become

Christian militants and missionaries, and that the clergy have the splendid and exciting job of training the laity for action. Mission cannot be delegated. It involves us all.

NOTES

1. Hendrik Kraemer, *A Theology of the Laity*, p. 24.
2. Yves M. J. Congar, *Jalons pour une théologie du laïcat*, p. 13; quoted by Kraemer, op. cit., p. 74.
3. Lesslie Newbigin, *One Body, One Gospel, One World*, p. 16.
4. Kraemer, op. cit., p. 114.
5. See Stephen Neill, *The Unfinished Task,* p. 125.
6. Roland Allen, *Missionary Method: St Paul's or Ours?*, p. 18.
7. Ibid., p. 23.
8. Ibid., p. 24.
9. Ibid., p. 116.
10. Ibid., p. 121-2.
11. Ibid., p. 161.
12. *Towards the Conversion of England*, p. 36 (1945).
13. *Part-Time Priests?*, ed. Robin Denniston, p. 23 (1960).
14. Ibid., p. 52.
15. Ibid., p. 101.
16. Ibid., p. 12.
17. A. G. Hebert, s.s.m., *The Church and the Life of Fellowship*, p. 13-14.
18. Cf. Douglas Webster's statement: "the form of the Church must be the form of a servant, utterly humble, unmistakably human and completely obedient . . . as an instrument of Mission the Church's only conceivable form is the form of a servant." (*Local Church and World Mission*, p. 47-48.) See also J. H. Oldham: "A revolution is needed in the present outlook of the Church. Instead of making itself the centre and appealing to those outside to attend its services and take part in its own institutional activities, it needs to concern itself in a new way with the struggles and problems of those of its members who are living in the real world and helping

by their daily decisions to direct its course." Dr Oldham quotes Professor Ernst Michel, a Roman Catholic layman, author of *Renovatio*: "there is only one place at which a genuine renewal of the life of the Church can take place, namely at the point at which its mission of transforming the world is being fulfilled. The only real renewal is a healing and saving manifestation of the power of love in open and courageous encounter with the world." (*Life is Commitment,* p. 90-91.)

19. J. C. Hoekendijk, *International Review of Missions,* 1952, p. 332; quoted by Stephen Neill in *The Unfinished Task,* p. 21.

20. Joseph Cardijn, *Challenge to Action,* p. 52; quoted by Alfred R. Shands in *The Liturgical Movement and the Local Church,* p. 54.

21. Georges Michonneau, *The Missionary Spirit in Parish Life,* p. 171; quoted by Shands, op. cit., p. 54.

9

Evangelism

TRAINING for mission must not be allowed to turn inwards into a series of meetings which become an end in themselves. Action must follow, and this action needs to be more than the advertising of services and parish activities. Around the worshipping community there is a great mass of nominal Christians and of those who have no allegiance to Christ at all. It is to them that we are sent, and we are to evangelize them. For the Christian message is not an exhortation to do good or to be good, it is the good news that in Christ we can be rescued. Training for mission which stops short of its most direct fulfilment in evangelism has not achieved its purpose, whatever incidental good may come of it.

The need to present the Gospel arises directly from the facts of the human situation. All men belong to God, but sin has separated us from him and from each other. God in Christ has taken action to rescue and restore us. When we have seen that the Cross bridges the gap between sinful men and a holy God, and when we ourselves have been reconciled to God by the acceptance of Christ as Saviour and Lord, then we are at once involved in the ministry of reconciliation. We can see, now, that the Gospel is good news for each particular person. We can see that it is our job to take this message out into the world.

Without evangelism the Church cannot grow: it is

doomed to senile decay and ultimately to death. However involved we are in the pastoral system, however concerned about the social implications of the Gospel, it is the presentation of the Gospel itself that is our primary and fundamental task. Evangelism is not a special or exceptional activity of the Christian community. God's redemptive activity is going on all the time, and the Church is the means he uses. There should be an evangelistic content and outreach in the ordinary, regular activities of every parish. There should be evangelistic preaching; there should be evangelism through parochial activities; and there should be evangelism through personal witness.

This is not a task that we have to tackle as isolated individuals. God has made us members one of another, and in the body of his Church we are to belong together, to grow together, and to show together the pattern of the new life in Christ. Mission is to be a constant reality as the local Christian community lives out the love of God in every part of the world's life. In this work of evangelism the laity must be trusted to take an active part. They must be trained. They must be used. The whole life of the parish, through its corporate worship and the ministry of word and sacrament, through the organizations which are cells in a living body, through the daily witness of its dedicated members, should be making an evangelistic impact on the district.

This does not mean, however, that there is no need for special and intensive times of mission. A Parish Mission, when for ten days or so all efforts are channelled in this one direction, can be the means of God's breaking through to heal and restore and to enable the whole congregation to be the vehicle of his purpose.[1] So, too, it is only against the essential background of permanent mission that the work of a special parish mission can be fully effective. Without this steady evangelism, special evangelism can actually become a danger. A parish may decide to have a mission. Before the mission, any attempt at evangelistic enterprise may be met with the suggestion : "Let's wait until the mission." After the mission, there may be a general tendency to say, "The mission is over," and to say it with a sigh of relief, as the well-worn patterns reappear after their temporary submersion.

But the truth is that a parish mission can only be a particular and temporary expression of *the* mission—the movement of God to the world through his Church. The special thing is not a substitute for the permanent thing : it is a point of concentration for it, like a magnifying-glass which brings to a focus the rays of the sun.

If this is not understood, parish missions will be attempted in circumstances where failure is almost certain. All the experts say, for example, that a mission is not a cure for a dead Church. The reason is obvious : far from sinking back with a sigh of relief, the parish must follow up the mission by welcoming those who have taken a step forward in Christian faith and commitment into a living fellowship which means business. New-born babies can't survive on a cold doorstep.

Nearly everybody who is involved in a parish mission approaches it with fear and trembling. The busy Rector becomes busier than ever. The people of the parish wonder what to expect. They have visions of Bible-punchers landing on their doorsteps and pursuing relentless conversations with all the embarrassing earnestness of Jehovah's Witnesses. The members of the "visiting team", meanwhile, on their way to the parish, are suffering agonies of apprehension. "Many men approach a Mission with feelings of depression and nervousness," wrote Canon Peter Green, one of the greatest of Anglican Missioners. He added : "I do myself. I seldom journey to the scene of a Mission without feeling sorry that I accepted the invitation to conduct it, and without thinking that if I get through all right this time I will drop taking Missions." [2] It is like the moment before a race, when the athlete swears he will never run again. But, says Peter Green, "by the end of the first or second day the depression has vanished."

The fact is that when we have realized that this is God's work, and not ours, and when we have learned to rest in him, to look to him, and to forget ourselves, things begin to happen that in our more faithless moments we could not have believed. The people who come forward to witness that they have trusted God in Christ are not (as had been feared) emotional girls, but mature men and women who needed only this direct call for commitment to bring a theoretical Christianity to life. Visiting and House Meetings, instead of being characterized by mutual embarrassment, become the occasions of real encounter and conversation. The mission team, in their daily briefing sessions, can be heard in paroxysms of Chestertonian laughter. The Brains Trust that they thought would flop because there would be no questions runs out of time, and people ask for more.

Often we are content with such a tentative and truncated version of the Gospel that we are surprised when God honours our faith and shows us what he can do when we trust him. But we must really trust him. There is a need in parish missions (as in all evangelism) that we should not be content to sow the seed of the Gospel vaguely and generally, as if from a helicopter : it must be planted in prepared soil, and we should expect results. We have to preach for a verdict, and people have to decide "Yes" or "No". To use another metaphor (one sanctioned by the highest authority), fishers of men are meant to *catch* men, not just to influence them. What should we think of an angler who said, "How many fish have I caught? Oh, I haven't *caught* any, but I've *influenced* quite a few." Teaching Missions have their place, but let us not imagine that they are a substitute for evangelism.

Canon Bryan Green writes, "The evangelistic mission has one simple, plain objective. It is, to use the hackneyed definition—well worn, but none better—'so to present Christ Jesus in the power of the Holy Spirit that men may come to put their trust in God through him, to accept him as their Saviour, and to serve him in the fellowship of his Church.' It is to win people to God through Christ, to bring them to conversion by preaching the Gospel, At such a mission there will, or course, be teaching; there will be some elementary apologetics, for to ignore the intellectual and to appeal simply to the emotions is disastrous; there will, of course, be some simple devotions. The results that we shall look for from such a mission will be definite conversions; if there are not these definite conversions, then as an evangelistic mission the enterprise has failed." [3]

We must realize what evangelism is not. "It is not trying to improve moral standards and personal conduct. It is not convincing men about the truth of the Gospel so that they can give intellectual assent. It is not discussion about Christianity as a way of life. It is not the formation of churchgoing habits or the promotion of more frequent attendance at Holy Communion. It is not the creation of an emotional impression. It is not setting the teaching of Christ over against our modern social problems. All these activities may well be activities of the Church, and are often handmaids of evangelism, but they are not, on their own, evangelism." Evangelism itself is "the definite offering of Christ to men and women as their Saviour and Master, with the decisive object of bringing them to accept him." [4]

This "preaching for a verdict" is such a demanding task that we sometimes think it is the job of a few specialists. It is true that there are people with a marked evangelistic gift. But many Christians can practise evangelism, and all should be willing to try. One of the greatest benefits brought to the Church through the Village Evangelists in England was this sense that many ordinary clergy and lay-people could be used by God in evangelism if only they would put themselves at his disposal.

"Any Christian Minister or layman can preach evangelistically. It is not a gift confined simply to the technical and professional evangelist. It is true that God gives excellencies to different people; one is at his best as a teacher, pastor or administrator and is less gifted for the work of an evangelist. 'There are in every generation a few people who have supremely the gift of bringing their hearers to the point where a personal decision to follow Christ is made : but, granted all that, it still remains true that the minister is ordained for the purpose of bringing men and women to Christ; if he is not doing it it is questionable whether he ought to be in the Ministry at all.' The Christian layman is in the same position. If he is a Christian he must be a witness to what the Gospel has done for him, and in declaring that message he is doing the work of an evangelist. It is no excuse to say, 'I have no special gift', for surely the gift to evangelize is a gift of the Spirit rather than a gift of nature." [5]

If we doubt the need for evangelism in our Churches

to-day, we have only to realize how readily we rest content with the people we have. In many of our town parishes, for example, there are considerable numbers of Jewish residents. Our Church has no specialized missionary work among Jews in South Africa; it is left to the parishes to preach Christ to them. This may well be the right way. Many of the experts would favour it. But do we, in fact, accept the responsibility?

What are we really *doing* about evangelism? William Temple felt that parishes should have their groups of lay-witnesses, who would be prepared to go off and help neighbouring parishes with no more embarrassment than if they were a visiting football-team. By 1951 Canon Bryan Green was able to point to a growing recognition every-where of the need for the laity to be trained for evangelism. It was being increasingly recognized by all thoughtful Christians, he considered, "that the future of Christianity and the evangelization of the world rests, under God, in the hands of ordinary Christian men and women and not primarily in those of the professional ministers". The corollory was obvious : "If this be true, then nothing is of more urgent importance at the present moment than the task of training the ordinary lay members of the Christian congregations to accept and discharge their responsibilities." [6]

But for all the increase of emphasis on the laity, it is doubtful whether there has been an increasing emphasis on evangelism. The mission of the laity is generally accepted. Alfred Shands writes of the "inner essence" of the parish—"that small group who give themselves completely to the task of discovering God's vocation for them in their given situation"—"We believe that the principal function of the minister to-day in terms of a missionary strategy is to build up this 'inner essence' of the parish. The mission of the parish is going to stand or fall on whether the clergy are spending time on this task of training the few in leadership." [7] "We need to take the training of the laity as seriously as we do the training of the clergy," says George Goyder. "It is absurd that we spend so much time and money on the latter and practically none on the former. Would we expect an army or navy to win battles if its officers alone were trained?" [8] Yet even where such training exists, it is not always evangelistic in its content and in its effect.

There are, however, lay-leadership courses where the aim is to send well-trained soldiers into the battle. In the deanery of Islington, in London, such courses have been in progress for the past ten years. In 1960 the then Rural Dean, the Reverend Maurice Wood, wrote: "We *have* the man-power to be the total ministry of the Church, but it is slumbering in the pews." He quoted the statement of the Lambeth Report, "Many of the laity are prepared to become agents of evangelism . . . if they are shown the way," and his comment was: "If every diocesan bishop held regular instruction courses to train his clergy in methods of training their laity in Christian witness and service, there could be such a revolution in the life of the Church, as suggested above in the Lambeth Report." [9]

If the necessary revolution is to take place in the parish, Mr Wood suggests, it must begin with the incumbent and the inner circle through the Parish Meeting. "The inner circle must be taught to pray together, trained in Christian doctrine and action together, and then trusted with real spiritual tasks together." [10]

In this particular deanery, the annual Lay Leadership courses cover training in Christian doctrine and devotion,

Bible reading and the Holy Communion, witness, visiting, and personal counselling. Then, through regular visiting, "the inner circle become the ambassadors to the congregation so that in time the congregation may become Christ's ambassadors to those who live in the parish." [11] An evangelistic Guest Service once a month on a Sunday evening provides a specific opportunity to present the challenge of response to Christ, and to follow it with instruction and personal counsel. A similar pattern of regular training and evangelism has been followed for some years at All Souls', Langham Place, under the leadership of the Reverend John Stott, while at St Katharine's Foundation Fr Groser has concentrated most effectively on the training of the laity for full involvement in the life of the world. It is in the light of experience that Mr Wood writes : " 'The supplementary ministry' may be a temporary expedient to deal with a particular set of circumstances. Nothing, however, can take the place of the whole people of God in every local church being a converted, committed, and equipped army of Christian workers in the parish, and in the places of work and play where Church members penetrate." [12]

It is clear that our calling involves more than the acquirement of evangelistic techniques. Evangelism is essential, and its sharp cutting edge must not be blunted, for the encounter between a man and Christ is the purpose of mission. But evangelism has to be seen in the context of a wider outgoing. For Christ is the Lord of all life. He is to be served in daily work at the kitchen sink and the factory bench, in the office and the laboratory, the class-room and the mine, the farm, the shop, the surgery, and the law-court. The whole of the world's life has to be penetrated, in order that it may be transformed.

NOTES

1. A phrase used by the Reverend L. T. J. Shapter in summing up the aim of a Parish Mission.
2. Peter Green, *Parochial Missions To-day,* P. 111.
3. Bryan Green, *The Practice of Evangelism,* p. 124.
4. *Schools of Evangelism* (1949), p. 1-2.
5. Bryan Green, *The Practice of Evangelism,* p. 86. The quotation is from Bishop Stephen Neill, *Evangelism as the Primary and Basic Responsibility of all Churches,* p. 3. The implications of the last phrase are fully developed by Roland Allen.
6. Op. cit., p. 246.
7. Alfred R. Shands, *The Liturgical Movement and the Local Church,* p. 31.
8. "The Use of the Laity" in *Part-Time Priests?,* Ed. Robin Denniston, p. 105.
9. "Trained Laymen" in *Part-Time Priests?,* p. 86-7. Lambeth Conference Report, 2. 113.
10. Op. cit. p. 88.
11. Ibid., p. 91.
12. Ibid., p. 92.

10

The Church's Mission in the World

THE Church has already penetrated the world at many points through the work of clergy and other full-time specialists. Often it has done this simply by following its people, as in the work of military chaplains, who become part of the life of a garrison in order that they may minister to the Church's members there. In time of war the chaplain goes where his men go. The Missions to Seamen is another example of specialized ministry to meet special needs. Port Chaplains devote their whole ministry to the needs of visiting sailors, and the success of their work depends upon their identification with these men in their particular calling.

The ministry of hospital chaplains and prison chaplains demonstrates very clearly the concern of Christ for people : the priest is alongside them in their need. And not only the priest. The social work of the Church covers a wide field, and the workers include prison-visitors, trained nurses, matrons, house-mothers, and youth-club leaders, together with great numbers of voluntary assistants. In all this social outreach the Religious Orders are making a large contribution. Hospitals and maternity homes, orphanages, clinics and crèches, clubs and social centres placed where the need is greatest—where poverty, overcrowding, and unemployment make a breeding-ground for crime—all these are embodiments of the Christian concern for persons in their total life.

There is, however, one field in which the Church in South Africa has so far done very little. In Britain, industrial chaplains have been bridging the gap between the worker and the Church, and specialist agencies such as the Industrial Christian Fellowship have helped to keep before the whole Church its responsibility for people in the factory and workshop, no less than in the suburb and the home. Some of the leeway lost at the time of the Industrial Revolution has been made up in Britain, where Anglicans have the undoubted advantage, as members of the Established Church, of a prior right of entry. In South Africa, with no such advantage, we have been slow to move into the factories and the mines.

The fact that the great mass of the labour-force is housed in the African locations, and that its members suffer all the strains and indignities of the migrant labour system, makes contact difficult. If we were to employ industrial chaplains or priest-workmen, many of them would have to be Africans, since they alone would be able to share the life of the majority of manual workers. Yet there may be places where a white or Coloured priest could get into the factories, if time could be spared from parochial responsibilities, or if the Church considered this work sufficiently important to set men apart for it. Perhaps the first need is a survey of what is already being done.

In France the Jocists and the worker-priests tried to change the parish so that its life could become more relevant to the need of the worker, and to reach the worker through extra-parochial efforts by identifying themselves with him. Anglicans have used some of the same methods, and there are a few clergy of the Church of England who work full-time in industry.[1] The Lambeth Conference of 1958 considered that "while the fully-trained and full-time priesthood is essential to the continuing life of the Church, there is no theological principle which forbids a suitable man from being ordained priest while continuing in his lay occupation."[2] In the diocese of Hong Kong there are as many supplementary priests as there are full-time clergy. One of these auxiliary priests—a superintending engineer—was called to be Assistant Bishop of Borneo. The diocese of Michigan has a number of supplementary priests, and men have also been ordained there to a permanent diaconate.

In the Presbyterian tradition, the Iona Community in Scotland has made a sustained attempt to reach man in his total life, and one of the results has been an invigorating stream of Christian social thinking by which the whole Church has benefited. At Taizé in France there is a community in the Reformed tradition but living under the Benedictine Rule, which includes some Lutherans and one American Episcopalian. As at Iona, ordained ministers and laymen share the communal life and mission.

Anglicans appear to have made a comparatively restricted and stylized use of supplementary ministries. The offices of sub-deacon, lay-reader, and catechist are of immense value—not least in South Africa; but we have had nothing so wide in its scope as the office of Elder in the Presbyterian tradition, nor have we produced the great variety of supplementary ministries characteristic of the Latin Church. Has there ever been an Anglican community comparable with the Little Brothers of Charles de Foucauld, who seek to identify themselves with the poor, grouping themselves in working fraternities supported by the wages of their members? It is worth recalling that in the early Church the ministry was permanent, but it was not normally professional—bishops, priests, and deacons earned their livings in many trades and callings.

Every method by which the Church reaches out through its ordained ministry and through full-time lay-workers can be of great value as a witness to the Church's concern for the whole of life, and as a training-ground in the real problems of industrial man. In South Africa, which is only now undergoing its Industrial Revolution, we must not lose the opportunities which were so often lost in Europe and America.

But this is only one approach to the problem, and to omit to approach it from the other end as well would be fatal. For the Church's penetration of the working world through specialist ministers can never replace the outreach of the laity. Rather, as clergy and laymen join hands from opposite ends of the tunnel, the whole Church will find itself involved. The experience of industrial chaplains and worker-priests will bring greater realism to the strategy of lay-witness. And the laity will not only learn, they will also lead.

This has been the experience of the Church in Germany. The Evangelical Academies, started in 1945, have become places of dialogue between the Church and the world. Through the Academies people of different occupations meet to discuss with representatives of the Church their everyday problems of belief and behaviour. The Academies define themselves as places of discourse, of fundamental rethinking and of research. The German *Kirchentag,* which began in 1949, is defined by Kraemer as "a large-scale effort to bring together the laity of all Churches in order to develop and express a new sense of responsibility for and in all the life-sectors of the world, and to educate the laity for a courageous and spiritually intelligent witness in the world." [3] Both the Academies and the *Kirchentag* seek to serve the institutional Church, while deeply critical of its introvert spirit. They are forcing the Church to realize that the laity is its spearhead in the world.

The dominant lesson of all these experiments is the need for *community*. We need a Christian fellowship in which clergy and laity share equally. It must be a community as relevant to the world of the second half of the twentieth century as monasticism was to the medieval world. Within a common life of work and worship, priest and layman will learn to talk the same language and to understand each other's vocation. Ecclesiasticism will fall into the background as mission is taken seriously.

It is only a very unreal ecclesiasticism that can foster the illusion that the Church is in the world only, or even chiefly, through its ordained ministers who occupy certain "frontier positions". The truth is that the Church is in the world chiefly in its lay members. The salt of the earth cannot remain in the salt-cellar even if it wants to : it is stirred into the stew of the world's life. This is a fact, and it is to be joyfully accepted. It is dangerously unrealistic to talk of the need to penetrate and permeate society when *we are there already*.

But *how effectively* are we there? Again, it is easy to be deluded. If there is no consciousness of mission in this permeation, and if the whole Church does not realize what it takes to make mission effective, the salt will lose its savour wherever it may be.

Signs of Renewal asks, "Is it realistic to say that the Church *is* in its laity fully in those spheres of the world (factories, shops, political parties, government agencies, etc.) where the real battles of the faith are being fought to-day?

Is it not rather true that laymen and laywomen become gradually absorbed by the world because they conform to the spirit, the criteria, the hopes of this world? Do not most of the Church-members live a schizophrenic life having two different sets of ethics, one for the private Sunday life and the other for their behaviour in the workaday world? Does the Christian remnant really *live* in the world to function there as the salt of the earth?" [4] Bishop Lesslie Newbigin says, "It is still hard to bring even keen and instructed churchmen to the point of seeing that the Church's life and witness, her encounter with the world and therefore her place of obedience, is precisely in the work of her lay members from Monday to Saturday." [5] Our conventional clericalism and ecclesiasticism must give way to a realistic understanding of the whole Church and its whole mission.

The Liturgical Movement has provided the means of this discovery and transition for many Christians. Through it we have learned to relate the Church's worship in the Holy Communion to the work which men barter for food and drink six days out of every seven. The altar, brought forward among the people, becomes again a table instead of a sideboard. The hours of Eucharistic worship are changed. Often they used to be arranged to suit dear old ladies, and it was hardly surprising if the parish family tended to consist chiefly of dear old ladies. Now there may be a lunch-hour Communion, or an evening Communion after work. And certainly the Eucharist on Sunday will be the central expression of the congregation's corporate life. In such a service, the action begins to make sense. The Gospel Procession becomes a token of our intention to bring this good news to the world. The Offertory Procession is a symbol of our share in the world's life being consecrated to God, not the chance meeting of ten cents and a decent bason.

It is thirty-seven years since Fr Hebert wrote prophetically: "the Church is not merely an organization to bring together a number of religious individuals . . . but a society with an organic life, such as is best described in metaphors drawn from living things—she is the Bride of Christ, she is our Mother, she is the Body of Christ, of which he is the Head and we are the members. These are things which very many of us are trying to learn how to say. And many of us are convinced that the apprehension of these things is closely connected with the recovery of the true place of the Holy Eucharist in the life of the Church. . . . When we have learned again to celebrate the Lord's Service thus—not as a devotional service for the inner circle of the faithful in the early morning, nor as a mid-morning act of devotion with no communicants except the priest, but making the Parish Eucharist with the communion of the people the central act of worship on every Sunday—that service will teach us, by our participation in it, the meaning of the Fellowship of the Body more effectively than all our books of theology." [6]

How right he was—and yet, how much still remains to be done. The fact of our dispersal in the world is no advantage if we are impotent and paralysed except when we withdraw into the institutional life of the Church, where our activity becomes a form of escape. There needs to be a two-way traffic between the altar and the factory bench.

The Liturgical Movement can never be an end in itself. If its tenets become a new orthodoxy they may harden our hearts as well as our ceremonial. It is only one instrument among many in the encounter between the Church and the world. Theological and sociological realities remain to be explored because we have been content with a superficial contact. It is no use paddling in the shallows of the world's life : we must plunge in at the deep end.

Kraemer writes : "An adequate view of the reality of the complicated world of to-day is perhaps for a Christian the best inducement to probe anew the depths of Christian belief, and to understand that the lay issue is not primarily a matter of well-organized action, but of a new grasp of the Christian Faith." [7] It is in the Western world, with its easy tolerance, that the danger of absorption and conformity is greatest. On this ground Kraemer argues that while in the Eastern world, under communist domination, the Church is in the most clearly challenging position, it is the Western world that is the most *dangerous* place for the Church to live in. The paradox of South African society is that while it reveals some of the menace of all totalitarian systems, Christianity is not only tolerated here : in theory, it is embraced by the State. The challenge is there, but there is also the danger of absorption and conformity. The two dangers do not cancel each other out; if the jackboot can kill, so can the bear-hug, and we are subjected to the pressures of both. Our tendency is to be modest and mediocre, when we should be adventurous and prophetic.

Christians affirm that this is God's world. We go out to meet Him *there*. He is there before us. We cannot as Christians behave as if God were left behind in church, where we shall meet with him again next week, when our spiritual batteries need re-charging. On the contrary, the whole world is the continuing concern of his love. It is in this world, with all its problems, that we have to demonstrate a community that overcomes the barriers of race and class, including the class-barrier between clergy and laity.

The world of daily work is not occupied only by men and women who work with their hands. Our outreach must include schools and universities, touching the particular spheres of the artist, the writer, the scientist, the teacher, the politician, the doctor, and the lawyer, as well as the whole field of business management. Specialist discussion-groups on the lines of the German Academies could begin in a small way. Already we have our school and university chaplaincies, but it is doubtful whether we are giving them the attention and the support that the situation demands.

Canon Alan Richardson, Professor of Theology in the University of Nottingham, points out that our secular society, "the modern Leviathan", can easily assimilate the products of a relatively small number of religious schools into the standardized mass-culture of our day. Yet he quotes Christopher Dawson in support of his thesis that it is precisely in the sphere of higher education that the Christian challenge to secularism can become effective. "The only part of Leviathan that is vulnerable is its brain, which is small in comparison with its vast and armoured bulk. If we could develop Christian higher education to a point at which it meets the attention of the average educated man in every field of thought, the situation would be radically changed." [8]

Among the measures necessary to achieve this would be the higher theological education of good graduates (clergy and laymen) to fill posts in schools, universities, and theological colleges; the constant relating of school life to society and its needs, and the avoidance of any tendency to let the school become a little world of its own; the provision of adequate support and equipment for university chaplaincies; and the relating of Christian thought, worship, and witness among students to parish life and to the whole life of the world.

The danger is that Leviathan will invade and neutralize our institutions unless we vigorously maintain their specific Christian character. Even at present a great deal could be done to bring the message of Christian faith and discipleship to young men and women in their formative years. In some of our universities, evangelistic missions—usually under combined sponsorship—have made a considerable impact. Teaching and evangelistic missions in our schools might be even more effective. It is not enough to possess these well-established schools : the question is whether they are producing dedicated and devoted Churchmen who in every walk of life will bear a Christian witness. Even more important than any sporadic ventures of evangelism is the constant day-to-day tone of the life of a school. Christian training in depth seems, somehow, to be eluding us. Too often we produce nice people, when we should be sending out informed and dedicated Christians.

"Only when the smithy is the church of the blacksmith, the ship the church of the sailor, the laboratory the church of the chemist, will a man be able to live without hindering others." Those words, quoted by Maxim Gorki in his diary, were spoken by a very odd character, a Russian doctor who chose to live for many years as a tramp. Such a man, no doubt, is slightly touched. But it may be that—like Francis of Assisi, and Brother Lawrence and Kagawa and Studdert Kennedy—he has been touched by the finger of God.

NOTES

1. See *Part-Time Priests?*, p. 134 ff.
2. *The Lambeth Conference.* Resolution 89, p. 1. 51.
3. Hendrik Kraemer, *A Theology of the Laity*, p. 40.
4. *Signs of Renewal*, (W.C.C.), p. 59; quoted by Kraemer, op. cit., p. 37.
5. Lesslie Newbigin, *One Body, One Gospel, One World*, p. 16.
6. A. G. Hebert, S.S.M., in *Liturgy and Society.*
7. Kraemer, op. cit., p. 44-45.
8. *The Church Times*, 3 November, 1961. Quotations from *The Historic Reality of Christian Culture"*. p. 88-89.

11

The Problem of Communication

"You see," said the Rector, "the fellowship of the Church is like that stained-glass window—it's all made up of little squares. You're a square, and I'm a square." The teenagers waited for him afterwards. "You speak for yourself," they told him.

This unfortunate misunderstanding—like the English Rector's reference to "this great succour", which so grievously offended the generous American millionaire—exemplifies something that is always happening : the speaker fails to make his point because, to the listener, his words mean something different.

It is hard for an older person to learn the special language of young people (as hard as it is for an Englishman to speak good American), and the result of such attempts often sounds forced and stilted. Invisible inverted commas make the words of the new vocabulary stand out, which is just what they were not meant to do. Besides, the fashion changes too quickly for the outsider ever to be quite up-to-date.

The best person to convey the Christian message to any group is someone who is himself a member of the group. This is one of the most important factors pointing to the need of a truly indigenous Church, whose members think and speak like those to whom they witness.

It should be added, however, that real and effective

identification can be made between the missionary or evangelist or witness and those to whom he is sent, even though differences may be wide at the beginning. This is one of the lessons of Christian history. It was a Jew who took the Gospel to Rome; a Roman who took it to France; a Frenchman who took it to Scandinavia; a Scandinavian who took it to Scotland; a Scotsman who evangelized Ireland, and an Irishman who in turn made the missionary conquest of Scotland. Sometimes the invitation to such identification comes from the other side. When people demand of us that we learn their language—as so often happens in South Africa— they may really be asking us to enter into their world in order that we can understand them. Sometimes, it is true, they may merely want us to conform to their pattern of life, and so confirm them in it, but it is not necessarily so.

In any case, without some measure of identification, there can be no communication of the Christian message. As Hugh Redwood put it, "To save a man for Christ we must not ram him and sink him : we must lay ourselves alongside him". Identification has its difficulties, but what we all have in common as members of a sinful humanity is immensely greater than any cultural or racial factors that may divide us, And the job we have to do is essentially simple. "Evangelism", says D. T. Niles, "is one beggar telling another beggar where to get bread."

Nevertheless, our problem is not just one of different ages and backgrounds and ways of speech : history has a hand in it too. The language of theology seems remote and foreign chiefly because it *is* remote and foreign : it is full of Greek and Latin words and ways of thinking. Liturgy and traditional devotion come to us in the language of the past, a language often beautiful, but sometimes more soothing than the truth it is meant to express: "In so general a manner and so sonorous a prose do we confess our sins that they scarcely seem sinful; and the flawlessly performed ceremonial . . . seems designed to transport us into an ideally comfortable world where there is nothing disquieting, unseemly or actual." [1]

Christians rightly value their history, with its majestic continuity of worship and devotion from the times of the Hebrew Psalmists until to-day. Yet there may be a danger that the padding of familiar phrases will absorb the impact of what God wants to say to us now. Many Church members, for example, while admitting that the Authorized Version of the Bible sounds archaic, will complain that modern translations are somehow "less than holy". Perhaps they are looking for a religion dignified and remote. Christianity is neither.

If the problem of communicating the Gospel so that ordinary people can understand it were simply a matter of words, it could be overcome by translation into current speech and by the use of witnesses whose familiarity with their milieu, whether inherent or acquired, would minimize misunderstandings. No doubt there would remain a necessary technical language of theology, which would have to be learned, and the Church would have every right to expect the enquirer to become familiar with special terms, as the novice at golf learns to talk of eagles and birdies. But what if the enquirer cannot even discover what game it is we are playing, or if he finds it so unreal that he no longer wants to know?

Here is the real problem. Behind the new language and the new ways of thinking of young people to-day there lies something more serious : a rejection of customary patterns of life. And this rejection, as Philippe Maury says, is a warning signal to the Church that its message is no longer reaching the world and that it must be presented in some new form.[2]

Theodore Wedel points out that "verbal presentations of the Gospel frequently find themselves giving answers to questions that have not been asked—or not asked as yet." [3] Should we not, therefore, begin where people are—begin, in fact, at the other end, with the questions people *actually* ask and the needs they really feel? That is to say, communication cannot be monologue, it must be *dialogue*. "The Church must once again be 'on speaking terms' with the world, because without this dialogue evangelism, mission, is impossible." [4]

Dialogue is undoubtedly a difficult process. Even in ordinary life, many conversations virtually consist of two inter-penetrating monologues. Each speaker only wants a passive listener. Christians who feel secure in the world of their familiar terminology may suspect that, for them, dialogue would be dangerous. Are they being asked to lose the initiative? Yet there is not much point in keeping the initiative if nobody understands what you say. Soon nobody will be listening. It is surely braver, and also more realistic, to start where people are, and to learn to meet *their* problems in words they understand.

The snag is that the Church cannot allow itself to be manoeuvred into the position where it becomes a mere agency to relieve tension, make people happy, and supply spiritual dynamic for the carrying out of society's projects. As Canon Demant says in *Theology of Society,* the Church should "cease trying to give a better answer than the world to the problems the world has set in its own way. It must take the problems men have and show that they are

9

insoluble unless they are restated in terms of the nature of the reality as the Christian faith knows it." [5]

D. T. Niles makes the same point : "We often talk about Jesus Christ as the answer to human problems. Jesus Christ is not the answer to our problems; he is the answer to the problems he raises in our lives. Jesus is not the answer to the questions which a Hindu asks; he is the answer to the questions which the Hindu ought to ask. Jesus must first make men ask the right questions before he becomes for them the answer. Again and again in our evangelistic work we shall discover that the problems of many people are not the problems Jesus came to answer. But he does raise certain questions, and when these questions become clamorous in the life of a person or of a group, they will find Jesus the only satisfying answer." [6]

For the Gospel to be relevant the Church *must* meet men where they are—"it must take the problems men have". But then there must be real dialogue, and not a mere acceptance of the world's own diagnosis of its ills. Monologue from the other side is no better than monologue from our side. George Macleod clearly recognized this tension when he wrote : "The task of mission is no more or less than to tell man who he is, with all that results from his hearing. The crisis of mission is so to tell him that he hears." [7]

Even when every effort of identification has been made, we have to recognize that the message may be refused. Essentially simple as the Christian Gospel is, there is something in it offensive to the natural man that makes it hard for him to accept. Maybe the beggar doesn't really want bread at all, but only a bottle of cheap wine. Kraemer points out that it was St Paul, that most fervent communicator of the Gospel, who emphasized the unacceptable, divine foolishness inherent in the message.[8] The Bible shows that even faithful and explicit communication can sometimes lead to a hardening of hearts. In fact, it is when things seem easy that we may have to be most critical of ourselves, for perhaps this too facile communication is the sign of a too complete accommodation to the world and assimilation by it : having learned the language, we may be using it to say sweet nothings.

We have been thinking of communication in terms of speech, but it would be a serious mistake to confine the problem to these terms. In the early Church, as Harnack finely said, "the new language of the Christians was the language of love in power and act".[9]

Florence Allshorn quotes the words of a young airman— words which show how relevant is the appeal of action in every age : "Don't try to help me or preach to me, or tell me what I ought to think yet. Don't work for my salvation, show me yours, show me it is possible, and the knowledge that something works will give me courage and belief in mine." [10]

This is a tremendous challenge to our Christian congregations to-day. Christian community and service are still the most effective ways by which the Christian faith can be communicated. When the phrase, "See how these Christians love one another", can again be said with amazement and admiration, and not as a sarcastic comment on our disunity, the language of deeds will make up for all our stammering.

What we do in church also has something to say. There is a language of ritual, and it either confirms or confuses the word we preach and seek to live. Our ritual may say one thing to the "insider" and something else to the "outsider". Ideally it should speak the same message to both, and it should be a message at once true to the biblical and historical revelation of God and vitally relevant to life in the everyday world. This is the great value of the Liturgical Movement: not that it is making us accurate antiquarians, but that it is helping ritual to communicate with life. Ritual which is fussy, and which becomes itself the focus of attention, has to be replaced by ritual which is meaningful and which moves the will as well as the emotions.

"Archaic forms of worship kill all evangelization", says Philippe Maury bluntly, "and it would be pointless to pursue a modern policy of evangelization, while preserving archaic forms of worship! This would lead to a kind of schizophrenia, and ultimately to spiritual death." [11] This is a bitter pill for Anglicans to swallow, and perhaps we ought not to swallow it; but it certainly calls for analysis, and a full report might show that it was good for us after all. Meanwhile, those who are experimenting with special forms of service for use in buildings other than churches deserve our understanding and support.

One of the most powerful media of communication is literature, and we shall consider this in the next chapter; but in addition to our use of books and magazines, Christians to-day are rightly concerned that the Church should use the great mass-media—films, radio, television, and the popular press—in the cause of Christ. It is clear that this will impose special disciplines and techniques which must be learned humbly and with a willingness to experiment. We do not seem to be very good about this. The usual broadcast of a Church service shows very little feeling for the medium. What is needed is surely something designed for radio and the listener, not for the church building and the churchgoer. This is a subject that calls for special and expert treatment.[12]

Here we must notice the effect of the *misuse* of the great mass-media of our time. When radio is used—as it very largely is in South Africa—to condition people and trivialize their thinking in the interests of propaganda and salesmanship, the effect is to add to the difficulties of all genuine and worth-while communication. It is the same with the cinema and the press. The verbal and visual images that bombard our senses daily are the tokens of a cultural disintegration. To-day there is no common world in which men feel at home. What we do have in common is that we all have to live in this confusing world, disintegrated as it is. This is the real challenge to the Church : to accept the actual situation, to face and enter the world as it is, this pagan world of our day.

Too often we want the Church to be a refuge from reality, and this desire we symbolize in buildings with thick walls, small windows, and medieval gloom, where we can play a game of "let's pretend". Kraemer writes : "The Church to-day lives in a secularized and disintegrated mass-society, which is unusually dynamic. It behaves, however, in many respects, as if it still lived in the old stable and parochial world." [13]

It would be a good exercise for Christians to-day to read, or if possible to see, the plays of Beckett, Adamov, Ionescu, Tardien, Pinter and N. F. Simpson. In these dramatists non-communication has become a cult—they are obsessed with man's impotence and disintegration. Their works have been vividly described as "screaming under water".[14]

From such plays one comes away with a powerful sense of man's nothingness and isolation. "Man without God is no longer man", said Berdyaev, and here we know it to be true. The value of these psychotic expressions of the condition of man to-day is not that they have any answer to offer, but that they make us realize that we who have the answer might also be accused of screaming—or perhaps muttering—under water, in a separate tank. Communication has broken down. The answer is not even more muttering in the murky depths. Yet much of our effort is directed into the tank instead of out beyond it.

There is an astonishing paradox in South African life. In many of our suburban parishes there is an almost nineteenth century air of accustomed religious observance, yet these parishes are set in a country of appalling problems, a country whose future is unpredictable. The intellectual revolt against Christianity in South Africa is too serious to ignore—yet we seem to be ignoring it. Kraemer argues that while the Church must identify itself with people, it must learn to live without indentification with any social structure. Objectively speaking, he contends, the Church as an institution is already in the melting-pot, though subjectively it has still not realized its predicament.[15]

There can be no solution by turning inwards. The end of that process would not be communication but mumbo-jumbo—the speaking of words and the performing of actions unreal to the world, and increasingly unreal to ourselves. So the problem of communication is not *fundamentally* a question of tactics or techniques. It is a question of trust and obedience. Kraemer, after a masterly analysis, calls upon the Church to show a robust faith in the power of the Holy Spirit, and so to discover that the continuity and the prestige it has been clinging to are merely crutches, without which it will stride out in the power of the forces inherent in its nature and its calling.[16]

Let the Church be true to its Lord, and it will speak for him in words and deeds. Above all, let the Church be *near* to its Lord. Dr T. F. Torrance stresses the fact that "because of the Incarnation and the creation of a new humanity in Christ, the Church is most relevant to the world as she keeps near Jesus Christ. She cannot discover her relevance by devising new methods of evangelism (needful as these may be) or by searching for points of contact, though the personal contact is of course supreme . . . The Church must above all rediscover the Gospel, and relearn the supreme relevance which it has to every human situation." [17]

It needs to be said, too, that we shall only learn to communicate the Gospel to the world of to-day by doing it—"the Churches must learn to speak the language of men by talking to them." [18] We have to begin, we have to try; and when we fall flat on our face we have to get up and go on again. Merely to discuss the problem is like talking about learning to walk, when you have no intention of putting one foot before the other.

NOTES

1. Raymond Mortimer, "Bishops", in *Turnstile One*.
2. Philippe Maury, "Christ's Ministry to the World", in *The Student World*, No. 1-2, 1961. p. 4.
3. Theodore Wedel, Foreword to *Man's Need and God's Action*, by Reuel L. Howe, p. viii.
4. Maury, op. cit., p. 5.
5. V. A. Demant, *Theology of Society*, p. 149; quoted by Kraemer in *The Communication of the Christian Faith*, p.92f.
6. D. T. Niles, "The Triune God, Mission and Unity", in *The Student World*, No 1-2, 1961, p. 45.
7. George Macleod, *Only One Way Left*, p. 41.
8. Hendrik Kraemer, *The Communication of the Christian Faith*, p. 29.
9. A. von Harnack, *The Mission and Expansion of Christianity in the First Three Centuries*, p. 173; quoted by Kraemer, op. cit., p. 39.
10. *The Notebooks of Florence Allshorn*, p. 16.
11. Maury, op. cit., p. 11.
12. The Diocese of Natal has appointed a Director of Public Relations, the Reverend Andrew Kay, and experiments are being made with a press advertising campaign as well as in the whole field of the proper use of the mass media of communication.
13. Kraemer, op. cit., p. 113.
14. A. Alvarez, "Audience of Captives", a review of *The Theatre of the Absurd*, by Martin Esslin in *The New Statesman*, 1 June, 1962, p. 798.
15. Kraemer, op. cit., p. 114.
16. Ibid., p. 115.
17. T. F. Torrance, *Conflict and Agreement in the Church*, Vol. 1, p. 223.
18. Maury, op. cit., p. 11.

12

Literature and Dialogue

CHRISTIANS have always set a high value on literacy because they are people of a Book. It has been one of the primary aims in all our missionary work to teach people to read, and then to give them the Bible in their own language. Anglicans have enough missionary experience of their own to appreciate why one of the world's greatest authorities on literacy should be a Christian missionary— Frank Laubach.

But it was Laubach himself who pointed out the *perils* of literacy, when he said it would have been better if we had never taught the people of the world to read unless we mean to go on and give them Christian books. John R. Mott declared that "the alphabet is the most dangerous weapon ever put in human hands". Mao Tse-Tung has provided a bitter commentary: "These Christians have done a great work in teaching the people of China to read; now it is for us to take advantage."

What are the world's new readers—and particularly the new readers of Africa—actually finding to read? The answer is, first, the products of the popular, commercial press; and then, political and ideological propaganda; and then, sectarian books and pamphlets, many of which present a version of Christianity profoundly distorted and heretical. The new readers of Africa are certainly reading. They are reading anything they can get. The tragedy is that we are so slow to follow up the Bible and the Prayer Book with *popular Christian literature* that will establish them in faith and sound knowledge. Our failure to do so amounts to a sheer waste of our educational pioneering.

One of the things that holds us back is the problem of translations. We are sensitive about language—perhaps too sensitive. We do not want to give the impression that the Anglican Communion is *Die Engelse Kerk*. But if we are to try to be multi-lingual in everything we produce, three points are worth noticing. First, a great many languages are spoken in South Africa, so it is not enough to be bilingual or tri-lingual. Secondly, multi-lingual papers and magazines do not succeed in South Africa. No single reader is satisfied. Each feels that he is missing something. Such papers tend to go into a decline and to suffer an early death. And thirdly, the popular magazines produced for the African market are often written in English. Some of these magazines have editions in various languages, but *Drum*, with its brilliant editors and writers and its outstanding success, is an English-medium magazine. English is understood by millions of people throughout the Province. We should not be ashamed to use it. And whatever happens, we must not allow the problem of many tongues to silence us.

It may be that we shall have to take more seriously the large Afrikaans readership in the Church of the Province, a readership that will grow further as Afrikaans is increasingly used in Bantu education. In fact, there is not much popular literature produced by the Church of the Province available in Afrikaans, apart from *What the Church has said* (a statement about Apartheid) and *A Dream comes True* (the story of the Charles Johnson Memorial Hospital). Yet the fact that Afrikaans is widely used in conducting services suggests an equally wide need for Afrikaans literature.

The African languages used by the Vernacular Literature Committee of the Church of the Province are Zulu, Xhosa, Sesuto, and Setswana. The Bible and at least parts of the Prayer Book are used in many other African languages as well, but it is not considered practicable to produce popular literature in them all—the potential readership is too small. In fact, the total list of our vernacular productions in recent years is not a long one. Baptism and marriage pamphlets are available in Sesuto, Setswana, Zulu, and Xhosa. *Preach the Word* has been translated into Sesuto and Xhosa. *The Christian Family* is available in Sesuto, and a children's service-book and some sermon-notes in Xhosa complete the list.

The Church's policy in vernacular literature is to place on the diocese the onus for publication. When a diocesan bishop has made his case for a particular book, it is the diocese that bears responsibility for its printing and distribution. The total cost is met by the Vernacular Literature Committee, which recovers all the proceeds from the sale of the book.

There are a number of books which have been written with a view to translation—for example, the *Key Books* produced by the United Society for Christian Literature. None of these has been translated in this Province so far. World Christian Books, edited by Bishop Stephen Neill, are freely available for translation. *The Christian Family* is one of these, and a few other titles are being translated into Sesuto and Zulu. For all the difficulties, we can hardly claim that this amounts to a serious attempt to make popular Christian literature available to our members.

But difficulties of translation are not our chief problem.

The real cause for alarm is that we do not see the *necessity* of filling the dangerous gap: we do not realize with sufficient force the immense potential for good of the printed page.

Other Churches and missionary agencies are not unaware of the need. The Presbyterians at Lovedale produce *The Outlook*: the Sudan Interior Mission has *African Challenge,* a colourful and attractive magazine which circulates in the Republic; the South Africa General Mission publishes *African Hope* and *African Advance,* the first for teachers, the second for more general use. The production of our new Provincial paper, *Seek,* is an encouraging sign, and the Provincial Publications Officer, the Reverend Donald Leavey, reports that out of the first 2,000 orders received, more than 1,000 came from Africans. The readers are there: it is up to the Church to provide literature which will be a method of mission.

Literature can be a medium of evangelism. It can also be an organ and expression of fellowship as it links together the Church's members scattered throughout the Province, and tells them what the Church is doing. The challenge and inspiration of the Church in action is a great incentive to the individual Christian and the local congregation, and an effective antidote to the wrong sort of parochialism. The whole Anglican body in the Province needs its channel of communication, so that it may be conscious of its calling. This is not unrelated to effective mission; in fact, it is essential to it.

When we turn from the Province to the parish, and look at what the Church is actually doing there, we can hardly be content. Most parishes produce their own magazine, and these parish magazines ought to provide a most useful method of reaching every Church member and a considerable number of outsiders as well. Yet they are often poorly produced and full of shattering trivialities, as Canon Findley has pointed out. He quotes two examples:

" . . .The most important news I have for you this month is the Annual Bazaar . . ."

". . .The great news this month is that my wife and I hope to sail for England at the end of this month. . ."

His comment is: "Now, of course, that could be understood in more senses than one. But note the use of the word 'news'. Could anyone ever imagine that to the Church was committed the Gospel—the best of all possible Good News. But no—the things that stand out this month are the Annual Bazaar and the Rector's long leave." [1]

What are we to make of this extraordinary anomaly? The Church has been a pioneer of education. She builds schools, and fights to retain them. She breaks down illiteracy, puts in a sustained effort to educate people— and then drops into their post-boxes productions that make the heathen laugh and the Christians rage furiously together.

We are almost equally bad about using the great numbers of fine Christian books which are available in English, many in paperback editions and therefore not expensive. Parish libraries are comparatively rare. Books are seldom seen on sale in the church porch or the church hall. Many Christians read a special book during Lent, but apart from this apparently penitential act their knowledge of the faith is allowed to remain static while the rest of their knowledge goes on developing. Yet an articulate Church will inevitably be a reading Church, a Church that has grasped the great truths of the Christian faith in the language of to-day, and is therefore able to express them.

Have we realized, too, that literature can be a most effective means of dialogue with the non-believer, the enquirer, the uncommitted man in the street? Millions of people, many of whom never went to church, nevertheless read the books of C. S. Lewis and Dorothy Sayers, and through those books Christ and his Church have come to them. Many intelligent agnostics would be glad to read books such as *Who moved the stone?* by Frank Morison, or C. E. M Joad's *The Present and Future of Religion* and *Recovery of Belief,* or Professor Coulson's *Science and Christian Belief.* A Christian should have books to lend— books which he has read himself and which he can discuss with his unconvinced and unconverted friends.

Apart from parish libraries and personal libraries, there are many public libraries in South Africa which might well be willing to add new books to their shelves if enough people asked for them. Sometimes the "Religion" section of these libraries is quite good. Sometimes it is pathetically inadequate and out-of-date. We ought to start using it, ask for more and better books, and see that others use it too.

Let us not be afraid of reading widely. The world Church, in its many different Christian traditions, has produced and is producing literature that can help us all. The insight and understanding of others whose perspective differs from our own can throw a flood of light on problems that we have ignored or found obscure. To-day there is a rich exchange of theological thinking, and we impoverish ourselves if we are too narrow to pick up a book that does not bear the imprimatur of a familiar author's or publisher's name and the assurance of a congenial and undisturbing point of view. Perhaps it is the other man—the unlikely man—who is saying just what we need to hear.

Dialogue may begin with books, but it must go on as living conversation. By distributing good magazines and having books available to lend and to sell, we shall put ourselves in contact with many people who are outside the reach of what they would call "conventional religion". We shall show the relevance of Christian faith to daily life —and first of all we shall realize it ourselves. For habitual piety soon becomes dull and deadly, and makes us dull and deadly, unless it is fertilized by fresh thinking.

Together with literature we need discussion—lots of it. In study-groups and cells there is something that is missing from many a parochial meeting where the faithful sit in rows to be addressed. The cell sits in a circle, and the faithful answer back. Some of the manifestations of the cell-movement, such as the Servants of Christ the King, are teaching us a new dependence on the Holy Spirit which is really as old as the Church itself, but which has been overlaid by generations of passivity.[2] Even in big conferences and conventions, which have their importance too, it is often the small discussion-groups rather than the plenary sessions that prove to be most fruitful and memorable.

Vocational groups and cells are perhaps the most stimulating of all. Here people can meet on a common level of experience, though perhaps with great differences of belief, to discuss the application of the Christian faith to their own calling. There may be a group of doctors, another of factory workers, another of teachers, another of housewives, and so on. It is a searching and a humbling thing to take part in such discussion, or to be a silent listener. Our cherished prejudices have to go. Bats are let out of belfries and skeletons emerge from cupboards. New ideas are shared and shaped, discoveries are made, old truths are burnished bright. A greater realism is an almost inevitable result.

In a famous chapter of his *Jesus of History,* T. R. Glover made the claim that the early Christians out-lived, out-died, and *out-thought* the pagans. He quoted the principle given by Clement of Alexandria : "The beautiful, wherever it is, is ours, because it came from our God." And so, he said, "The Christian read the best books, assimilated them, and lived the freest intellectual life that the world had." The inference is still valid : "There is no place for an ignorant Christian". The relevance of literacy to mission is unmistakably clear : "From the very start every Christian had to know and to understand, and he had to read the Gospels; he had to be able to give the reason for his faith. He was committed to a great propaganda, to the preaching of Jesus, and he had to preach with penetration and appeal." [3] This is still true to-day. Mission demands that we love the Lord our God with all our mind.

NOTES

1. Canon F. Findley, "On Parish Magazines", in *Good Hope,* July, 1962.
2. The origin and development of S.C.K. are described in Roger Lloyd's book, *Adventure in Discipleship.* There are a number of S.C.K. Companies in South Africa.
3. T. R. Glover, *The Jesus of History,* p. 216-7.

13

Unity, Renewal, and Mission

THE Mission of the Church and the unity of the Church are indissolubly connected in the great High-Priestly Prayer of Our Lord, ". . . that they all may be one, that the world may believe" (John 17. 21).

That they all may be one . . . We sometimes try to mitigate the force of that petition by spiritualizing it away. We like to make the point that there is a unity of spirit between Christians of different traditions, whatever physical divisions may exist. But what should we think of a divorced couple who claimed that after all they enjoyed *spiritual* unity?

The fact is that Christianity is not a religion of pure spirit. As someone expressed it, Christ did not communicate with the world by a disembodied voice crackling through some spiritualist trumpet : he took flesh. And when he commissioned his disciples he said, "As the Father hath sent me, *even so* send I you." Through them his ministry of incarnate love was to be continued : as Christ was in Galilee, so the Church was to be in the world. The unity he prayed for was a living, organic unity, not some vague bond of sympathy between dismembered parts.

And it was unity with a purpose : ". . . *that the world may believe*". The world will not believe until it sees spiritual unity take flesh. For our world is a world intensely divided, and how can it be saved by a Church whose divisions are as real and deep as its own? "When the world lies broken and half-dead by the side of the road it will not be helped much by a Church lying broken and half-dead on the other side of the road." [1]

Our easy acceptance of Christian disunity is perhaps the greatest single obstacle to effective mission to-day. When we study the Church in the Bible we cannot escape the conclusion that the Church is a called and appointed community which is to be the bearer of God's covenant and promise and to embody his saving purpose for mankind. Because of the unfaithfulness of the Old Israel, God narrowed down its dimensions to those of the Faithful Remnant, until at last we see his purpose embodied in a single personality, Jesus Christ. From that central point the pattern widens out again—Professor Leonard Hodgson liked to teach his students to visualize it in the shape of an hour-glass. Christ forms a community of twelve, the nucleus of the New Israel. The purpose is the same; it contains the elements of assembly and mission familiar in the story of the Old Testament Church: "He chose twelve, that they might be *with Him,* and that he might *send them forth*" (Mark 3. 14). Their unity with each other and with him is pictured in the symbols of the vine and the branches and the shepherd and the flock (John 15; 10). The ultimate purpose is that the whole creation should find its fulfilment in God.

At Pentecost God's Holy Spirit is given to the assembled believers, and from this time a new divine power directs their corporate life. All who confess Christ as Lord—of whatever race or tongue—are banded together in a loving, worshipping, serving, witnessing, and expectant fellowship.[2] Acts 2. 42 provides a classic summary: "They continued stedfastly in the Apostles' doctrine, and fellowship, in the breaking of bread, and in the prayers . . . and the Lord added to them daily."

The important thing about the New Testament Church is not that it is a local assembly, but that it is the people of God who are heirs of his promises.[3] The local Church is always the embodiment of this *universal* Church. It is not that the local Churches are added together to make up the great Church : rather, the Church is to be found *here* and *here* and *here*. St Paul never speaks of "the Corinthian Church", always of "the Church which is in Corinth" : it is the universal Church in its local embodiment.[4] And so he can write of the Church as the Body of Christ—his means of expression in the world.

To turn from the Church in the Bible to the Church as we see it to-day is like moving into an Alice in Wonderland world where nothing is quite what it seems. There, in the Bible, schism is an unthinkable sin—"Is Christ divided?" (1 Cor. 1. 13). Here, to-day, it is an accepted fact. There, the Church is a single sword in the hand of God; here, it is a handful of penknives.[5] Western missionaries brought to Africa a divided Church, and Africans learned the lesson all too well. We are saddened by the ever-increasing divisions of Zionism, but it is even sadder to realize that the origins of African Zionism can be traced to an apocalyptic sect in Zion City, Illinois—a sect which eventually split up into six different American groups. Even to-day the Bantu prophets with their 2,200 sects can point out that there are many more separatist churches in America— perhaps 36,000. Dr Sundkler believes that Zionism is caused chiefly by the colour bar *and by Protestant denominationalism,* and he holds that it cannot be dealt with effectively by a divided Church.[6]

The only argument we need for Christian unity is that it is the will of our Lord. But perhaps the force of this argument only comes home to our consciences when we wake up to the reality of God's purpose for his people to-day. So long as we imagine that we exist for ourselves we can be complacent—but only so long. Bishop Lesslie Newbigin says : "It is not possible to account for the contentment with the divisions of the Church except on the basis of a loss of the conviction that the Church exists to bring all men to Christ. There is the closest possible connection between the acceptance of the missionary obligation and the acceptance of the obligation of unity." [7]

It is not only in Christ's great prayer that mission and unity are connected : they are connected in recent history too. This is no accident : John 17. 21 provided the inspiration for the Ecumenical Movement, and was taken as a motto by young and vigorous movements within it, such as the international Y.M.C.A. and the World Student Christian Federation.[8] The Ecumenical Movement arose out of the missionary movement. As Bishop Wilson Cash put it, "God allowed a divided Church to evangelize the world, and in doing so it discovered that its divisions are intolerable." [9] The policy of comity was the beginning of co-operation, but it could not be the end. It led to the World Missionary Conference at Edinburgh in 1910, and on to the long process culminating in the foundation of the World Council of Churches in 1948, and to the fusion of the International Missionary Council and the World Council in 1961. The same process that brought the Church of South India into being is now at work in North India, Ceylon, Nigeria, Iran, and many other places. It is moving most resolutely where mission is taken most seriously, and it will never end until the prayer of Christ is fulfilled.

Every attempt to grapple with the realities of mission leads us to see the need for Christian co-operation, and, beyond that, the need of Christian unity. The Churchman in a factory thinks himself alone—but baptized Christians of different traditions are there too, equally powerless because equally isolated. Together they could do something: "the lay ministry shouts for the ecumenical Church".[10]

We have seen how a serious approach to the ministry of the laity leads us to consider the total structure of the Church, and we cannot confine this consideration to the limits of one ecclesiastical tradition. Kraemer's argument is that the possibility of revival and reform is inseparable from a serious consideration of the theology of the laity. We need to break out of our institutional thinking so that we can give first place to the conception of the Church as an ever-renewed adventure of faith, a response to God's great acts of salvation, redemption, and reconciliation.[11] "The issue is not that, if the laity were only given the opportunity and the right to do so, they would come to the rescue of the Church. The issue is that both laity and ministry stand in need of a new vision of the nature and calling of the Church and their *distinctive places* in it, which means conversion and reformation for the whole Church, laity as well as ministry." [12] Can we seriously maintain that this conversion and reformation have no connection with our unhappy divisions?

In the same way, our evangelistic efforts will remain isolated exploits unless the Church itself is prepared to change. Exciting and worth-while as they are in themselves, they point to the need for something more, for the Church's life of fellowship and service must reflect the Word proclaimed. Facing the fact of a divided and Christless world, the Lambeth Conference of 1958 said this: "To proclaim effectively the Gospel of God's reconciling love to the world, the Church must manifest in its own life the healing and reconciling power of the word it preaches." [13]

So, too, on the widest scale, the Christian missionary outreach calls for Christian unity. How can the eight hundred million baptized Christians in the world be mobilized for action? The appeal of the isolated pioneer-adventurer seems hopelessly dated to-day. It is only when preparing for a fancy-dress party or a University Rag that people now think of a missionary as a man with a sola topee and high button boots who treads through steaming jungles. The slogan "Doctor Livingstone I consume", on a float with savages dancing round a missionary in a cooking pot, can raise a smile in a generation which does not know the great words of a great man : "The spirit of Missions is the spirit of our Master . . . God had an only Son, and he was a missionary." Even John R. Mott's great challenge, "The evangelization of the world in this generation", has a dying fall in a disillusioned and divided world which lives under the ever-present threat of atomic annihilation. But men and women to-day can catch a new vision when they realize that the Christian world-mission holds the secret of unity—that it can make mankind one family. "One Body, One Gospel, One World"—this may be the theme demanded by our situation : a theme that will find an answer in the hearts and consciences of Christian people.[14]

Looking at the New Testament picture of the Church, Christians often ask plaintively, "Is there a way back?" The answer must surely be "No", for God has set his seal on history, and Christians have to take history seriously. Every attempt to *jump* back into the New Testament world only creates another schism, another separation. The purified Church soon becomes institutional, and then another withdrawal is called for—another flight from reality. It is in circles where the cry "Back to the Bible" is most vociferous that schism proliferates like microscopic life in a stagnant pool.

Nor is there any way back by the *acceptance* of division and the pretence that it does not matter because what we have in common is more important than what divides us. Fundamentalists who feel a deep unity with one another across the barriers of denomination are often strongly opposed to the Ecumenical Movement. They feel they already have the only unity that matters. The result of this fundamentalist loyalty, however, is to introduce a great horizontal cleft right through the vertically divided denominations. Each tradition now has its fundamentalist and its non-fundamentalist section, and in addition there is an unchurched multitude of individualist Christians, to make confusion worse confounded. It is true, of course, that all Christians—and not only fundamentalists — have a great deal in common, but this makes our divisions more scandalous, not less.

There is no way back : *but there is a way forward*. This way is to accept the mission of the Church, with all that it demands. Until we do that, our tentative approaches to reunion will be slow and reluctant and half-hearted. But when the Holy Spirit has set us on fire with missionary zeal we shall really move, and the cause of unity will come alive. For when we take mission seriously, we cannot be content to belong to introverted religious clubs; we must be, and be seen to be, members of the Body of Christ.

141

The goal of unity, like the goal of mission, is reached by taking particular steps. What steps can we take? In South Africa, our differences of colour, culture, and language have put a brake on every sort of togetherness. Spiritual isolationism has flourished in the general atmosphere of suspicion and separation. There has never been any well-developed comity in South Africa, despite consultations among missions and between Churches. Yet Christian congregations can move forward as they pray and work for unity. One great factor drawing us together is the prayer already offered by many Christians of different traditions, for that unity which is Christ's will for his Church.

When we get up from our knees, there are other things we can do. We can know our own traditions well enough to communicate them. We can meet together and learn to know each other. We can be willing to discover what others really believe, and to pension off our old stereotypes of Papists and Protestants in the light of a living encounter. Occasional united services, exchange of pulpits, and the meetings of Ministers' Fraternals are not to be despised. And where mission comes alive there will spring up inter-denominational groups working on specific problems of witness in the modern world. There are some social projects, too, that could be tackled more effectively together than separately; for example, the prevention of juvenile delinquency, or the care of old people.

We have noticed the Church's comparative neglect of mission to industry, and the difficulty of a unilateral approach. If Anglicans want to go into a factory, they will be told, "If we let you in, we must let all the others in as well." Why not go in *together*? It is reported from Australia that industrial missionary technique is being developed there as an inter-Church act of service by the Australian Trade and Industrial Mission (ATIM), which has contacts with the Anglican, Roman, Presbyterian, and Methodist Churches. "Inter-Church Industry Committees in Sydney, Melbourne, and Adelaide have included the member churches of the Australian Council of Churches and also the Roman Catholic and the Baptist Churches. ATIM has contacts with the Industrial Mission in Kyoto, Japan, with the Anglican Industrial Mission in Sheffield, with the Presbyterian Community of Iona in Scotland, with the Luton Methodist Centre, and with Catholic Action." [15]

Local co-operation is not enough, and for this reason the foundation of the Federal Theological Seminary at Alice in the Cape is a particularly important step. It should make possible a steady, permanent growth of understanding at the ministerial level. In the same way, specific discussions and consultations between Churches are more likely to be effective when they are backed up by common membership of bodies such as the Christian Council of South Africa and the World Council of Churches. And in a country as big and as thinly-populated as South Africa there is almost certainly a need for some *regional* embodiment of ecumenical thought and action, to bridge the gap between the local Church and the national and international ecumenical agencies.

These are steps on the way, but they are not the goal. The goal is organic unity, and it must not be purchased at the price of truth. Those who sneer at the idea of reunion as a sort of ecclesiastical rissole or shepherd's pie have missed the whole point that mission, unity, and renewal belong together. There is no question of uniting on the basis of a lowest common denominator—"You give up believer's baptism and we'll give up bishops." A united Church is not the same as "undenominationalism," which

Bishop Walter Carey aptly describes as "the dregs of that anaemic residuum of conflicting sectarianisms." [16]

The opponents of a sentimental or superficial unity are right. God in his mercy has given to the divided Church to discover and embody aspects of the truth, and these must not be lost. The one Church which is his will is to be the means of bringing all these aspects into harmony and completeness. For God has greater things for his Church than we have yet seen. The diverse riches which have been ours in isolation shall now be ours together, and the great Church-that-is-to-be will be immensely richer than the parts or even than the sum of them.

When we think of greatness and enrichment they are not to be conceived in terms of worldly power, but rather in contrast to little-mindedness and poverty of expression, for what we seek is not dull uniformity and drab mediocrity, but great variety within a common corporate life. It is very much easier to go on as we are, and only a great incentive will bring us to the point where we willingly face the sustained discipline that unity demands. The missionary challenge is the incentive we need.

Bishop Stephen Bayne, Executive Officer of the Anglican Communion, has expressed the conviction that the only worthy aim is the proclamation of the whole Gospel to the whole world by the whole Church, in these words : "The vocation of Anglicanism is, ultimately, to disappear. That is its vocation precisely because Anglicanism does not believe in itself but it believes only in the Catholic Church of Christ; therefore it is for ever restless until it finds its place in that One Body." [17] This is the restlessness of those who take seriously Christ's own prayer for the unity of Christians. This is the conviction of those for whom mission is not an option, but an obligation.

144

NOTES

1. Dr Douglas Horton; from an address during the closing service of the Third World Conference on Faith and Order, Lund, 1952.

2. See article: "Church", in *A Handbook of Christian Theology*, p. 60ff.

3. See article: "Church", in *A Theological Word Book of the Bible*, p. 46ff.

4. Ibid., p. 48.

5. This quotation has proved difficult to trace, though Bishop E. S. Woods expressed himself similarly in *How Stands Reunion?*, p. 6: "The forces of good and evil are everywhere locked in a mighty struggle, but the Christian Church is not a single sword in the Hand of God."

6. See *Bantu Prophets in South Africa*, p. 48, 53-4. 295, 301.

7. Lesslie Newbigin, *The Reunion of the Church*, p. 11.

8. "The inspiration of the Movement is beyond dispute. It can be found in what Temple described as 'perhaps the most sacred passage even in the four Gospels—the record of the Lord's prayer of self-dedication as it lived in the memory and imagination of His most intimate friend'." (F. A. Iremonger, *William Temple*, p. 389.)

9. See W. Wilson Cash, *The Missionary Church*.

10. Emma Lou Benignus, "The Laity Today" in *Viewpoints*, 1959.

11. Hendrik Kraemer, *A Theology of the Laity*, p. 87.

12. Ibid. p. 95.

13. *The Lambeth Conference*, 1958, p. 2.20.

14. See Lesslie Newbigin, *One Body, One Gospel, One World*, p. 12f.

15. *The Church Times*, 14 September, 1962, p. 3.

16. Walter Carey, *The Church of England's Hour*, p. 65.

17. Bishop Stephen Bayne, in *Pan Anglican* for Epiphany, 1954; quoted in *Lambeth and our Times*, p. 12.

Summing-up

To think about methods of mission, however inadequately, is to be faced by clear demands, and some of these are implicit in the main points which stand out from all that we have been considering. Let us sum them up.

Mission is the most important job in the world.

It is laid upon every Christian because it is laid upon the whole Church.

The whole life of the Church in every place is the agency of God's redemptive purpose.

Laymen have played a large part in the modern missionary movement.

The growth of the Church has been spontaneous rather than strategically planned, and in this growth the active witness of individual Christians has been indispensable.

Christian institutions do not solve the problem of mission, they only provide a means of mission. Institutionalism must not be allowed to make us inward-looking and socially conservative.

The Church is called to bear a prophetic witness in the political and social sphere: it must be a Confessing Church, whatever the cost.

Paternalism has to be replaced by a fellowship in which Christian community can thrive, and in such a fellowship race will be irrelevant as a criterion.

We dare not ignore our direct responsibility to preach the Gospel to the heathen.

The fulfilment of the Church's mission lays upon us the necessity of prayer; of the calling-out and training of men and women from within our own Province; of the proper provision and use of money; of a vigorous intention to penetrate and evangelize society; and of Province-wide co-ordination of effort.

It is in the parishes that partnership in mission needs to be realized, that missionary education must take place, and that mission itself is to be practised.

The laity are the primary agents of mission, and the main area of that mission is the world where they live and work.

The Church never outlives the need for evangelism, which should be a regular activity everywhere, involving the committed Christian nucleus of every parish.

The Church has to penetrate the working world through special agents and agencies, but even more important is the witness of its members in their places of work, for in them the Church is there already.

We have to take seriously the problems of identification and communication, so that the Gospel can be understood, and this we can only do as we go out to make contact and enter into dialogue with others.

Literature is a vitally important means of communication, dialogue, and mission.

Effective mission calls for Christian unity, in fulfilment of Christ's prayer, ". . . that they all may be one, that the world may believe."

These demands are enough to drive us to our knees; and this, surely, is what God wants first and most of all.

There is only one more thing to say : this matter is urgent. As the Archbishop of Cape Town has put it, "time is *not* on our side. . . If the Church in South Africa is to bring the Province to the feet of Christ, it must be done now." [1] For already the human family in South Africa has split into extremes of mutual rejection. In such a situation people are not ruled by reason. Events move too fast, conscience has too small a voice. People are forced to take sides, and then to listen only to the voices of their own side.

But Christians are committed to a Church that is bigger than race, to a Lord who is for all mankind. Christians belong together, and cannot accept the logic of a mad little world of men. They may be hated and hunted for it, and some will give in, taking the easy way. It is those in whose lives Christ is deeply at work who will not let go the truth; and he who is the Truth will not let go of them. They will be the prophets and witnesses of a better future. Even if there are few who listen, they will still be right. As Dr Edgar Brookes has put it, "We need not, even in our direst extremity, *wait* for the triumph of God in the world. It is already here wherever loving, trusting, and pure hearts are to be found. The times and seasons are with God—his Kingdom is within us. The light shines in darkness and the darkness overcomes it not : it never will." [2] When radar was being developed in 1936 in face of the threat of the second world war, Sir Robert Watson Watt coined the slogan, "Every week that passes is one per cent of the time we can count our own." He was not far wrong. Are we, perhaps, behaving as though we had an indefinite allowance of time? The early Christians were even less inclined than the pioneer of radar to trade on the future. They learned to live in daily expectation of their Lord's return, so that mission could never be postponed—the accepted time was *now*.

For the Church to be ineffective it is enough that we should go slightly off-course—put our own ease and comfort first, relegate our primary purpose to some secondary agenda for future consideration. That deviation will be enough to keep us orbiting in outer space for ever.

NOTES

1. Article in *The Church Times*, 20 July, 1962. A reprint is available from the Provincial Publications Office, P.O. Box 1932, Cape Town.
2. Edgar Brookes, *The City of God and the Politics of Crisis*, p. 8.

For further reading

From the great number of books available on this subject a few are suggested here in addition to those referred to in the notes. Some of these books contain more detailed bibliographies.

CHAPTERS 1-6

God's Kingdom and Ours   A. G. Hebert   S.C.M.

The Renewal of the Church   Visser 't Hooft   S.C.M.

The Mission of the People of God   L. S. Hunter   S.P.C.K.

Towards a Theology of Mission   Wilhelm Andersen   S.P.C.K.

The Theology of the Christian Mission   Ed. G. H. Anderson   S.C.M.

The Christian Mission   M. A. C. Warren   S.C.M.

Message and Mission   E. A. Nida   Hamish Hamilton

Christian Missions and the Judgement of God   David M. Paton   S.C.M.

The Missionary Church in East and West   Ed. Charles C. West and David M. Paton   S.C.M.

The Mission of the Anglican Communion   E. R. Morgan and Roger Lloyd   S.P.C.K.

The Anglican Church in South Africa   Peter Hinchliff
Darton, Longman & Todd

The Christian Ministry in Africa   Bengt Sundkler
S.C.M.

The Man Next to Me   Anthony Barker   Fontana

Black Woman in Search of God   Mia Brandel-Syrier
Lutterworth

Christianity in Africa   Cecil Northcott   S.C.M.

*The Primal Vision—Christian Presence ami. African
Religion*   J. V. Taylor   S.C.M.

CHAPTERS 7-13

The Parish in Action   Joost de Blank   Mowbrays

Revolution in a City Parish   Georges Michonneau
Blackfriars

The Parish Seeks the Way   Michael Hocking
Mowbrays

The Parish Comes Alive   E. W. Southcott   Mowbrays

Lay people in the Church   Yves M. J. Congar
Chapman

What is Evangelism?   Douglas Webster   Highway

Go Quickly and Tell   Augustine Hoey   Faith Press

Liturgy Coming to Life   J. A. T. Robinson   Mowbrays

The Parish Communion To-day   Ed. David M. Paton
S.P.C.K.

Crisis in Communication   Martin Boyd   S.P.C.K.

Christian Action in Society   W.C.C.

The Household of God   Lesslie Newbigin   S.C.M.

The Ecumenical Movement   Kenneth Slack   E.H.P.

*One Great Ground of Hope—Christian Missions and
Christian Unity*   Henry P. Van Dusen   Lutterworth